OTHER GOSPELS

by

PAUL B. SMITH, B.A.

Minister of The Peoples Church, Toronto

Foreword by
W. DOUGLAS HALL, ARTS/BUS. ADMIN.

MARSHALL, MORGAN & SCOTT
London

MARSHALL, MORGAN & SCOTT, LTD.
BLUNDELL HOUSE
GOODWOOD ROAD
LONDON, S.E.14

AUSTRALIA
119 BURWOOD ROAD
BURWOOD
VICTORIA 3125

NEW ZEALAND
3 CAMPBELL ROAD, BOX 24053
ROYAL OAK, AUCKLAND

SOUTH AFRICA
33 CENTRAL AVENUE, BOX 17
PINELANDS
CAPE

CANADA
HOME EVANGEL BOOKS LTD.
25 HOBSON AVENUE
TORONTO 16
ONTARIO

THE PEOPLES CHURCH, TORONTO
374 SHEPPARD AVE. EAST
WILLOWDALE
ONTARIO

U.S.A.
GOSPEL ADVANCE PRESS
P.O. BOX 2366, DENVER
COLORADO 80201

ISBN 0 551 05256 2

Typesetting by Print Origination Liverpool England

*Printed Offset Litho in Great Britain by
Cox & Wyman Ltd, London, Fakenham and Reading*

FOREWORD

Whenever something different is attempted crowds gather. All types are attracted. There are those who don't participate but are on hand just the same. They sit back smugly and wait for the expected disaster. Others, who prefer the "status quo" reserve judgement and are content to just wait and watch. The most interesting, however, are those who rise to the occasion and enjoy the stimulus of something new.

In his career as Canada's most exciting Evangelical Minister, Paul Smith has elicited all three responses more times in a year than most groups of ministers muster in a lifetime.

As Minister of The Peoples Church, Toronto—Canada's largest Protestant church—he packs its more than 2,500-seat auditorium Sunday after Sunday by taking calculated chances.

He once told me, "We're in the business of people. Without people, we're out of business. It's just that simple." With such a philosophy he has kept his ministry and church growing instead of either holding the line or seeing it fade into marginal or complete non-existence.

In the fall of 1967 I was personally involved with Paul Smith in what has become one of his most exciting and controversial "programs." As Director of Information for The Peoples Church, the two of us worked closely for months in the preparation, promotion and mechanics of a series he entitled, "What's the Difference?".

Years ago it would probably be called "The False

Cults and What They Believe" but this time it was different. Instead of the old-line attacks on other beliefs, the series was positive. The various points of view were to be stated clearly, objectively and most important of all, without shading—a rare accomplishment. The listener was to be left to make up his own mind.

Up to this point in the history of The Peoples Church, or any other for that matter, the problem of the so-called "false cults" was handled in a very uniform manner. The minister attempted to outline the various tenets and then preached on why he believed they were in error.

Paul Smith came up with the idea of inviting the leaders or appointed spokesmen into the church and letting them tell the congregation exactly what they believed and why they were not Evangelicals. So that complete freedom could be guaranteed and it would not be construed as an ecumenical cooperative programme, they spoke to an open meeting. There was just a brief introduction, no prayers, no hymns, no evaluation. The men were invited to address the congregation for twenty minutes with no strings attached.

With these guidelines the various groups were contacted. These included Roman Catholics (a Monsignor accepted), Christian Scientists, Spiritualists, Mormons, Modernists and Unitarians.

These gracious and articulate gentlemen welcomed the opportunity and appeared before packed congregations. Up to this point most of the audience had never really heard a forthright statement about the various beliefs. Following each address the guest left the platform and the evening service began. Paul Smith then preached, as many say, as he's never preached before, on the Evangelical position in the light of what had been said in the open meeting. It must be pointed out that his messages were not attacks. He made it quite clear that he did not have to go on the offensive or defensive. These men didn't attack the Evangelical position and he wasn't about to openly attack theirs. Despite what some may have thought, he didn't highlight the sameness between the beliefs, rather he pointed out the differences. This was all that was necessary for the majority who attended the series of meetings. The results were beyond expectations. Crowds were attracted and the faithbuilding and spiritual gains are still being felt in the church. Instead of being afraid to hear someone else's point of view the reverse was the case. For the first time, in many instances, Evangelical Christians graphically realized that what they believed could stand up against any other concept and stand up very well.

The idea has not ended with that one series. Other ministers in both Canada and the United States have tried it with varying degrees of success. This is a compliment to Paul Smith who was the first to do something different in the vital area of church doctrine.

Paul Smith carries this excitement over into his writings as well. *Other Gospels* which is an extension of this series, is not a rehash of the time-worn Evangelical critiques on the "false cults". Rather, it is a scholarly, objective outline and discussion of the entire subject. No personal bias shows through and for this reason alone the work is unique.

Paul Smith has also avoided the pitfall of glossing over marginal facts or suppositions by being subjective. If he makes a statement, he backs it up with incontestible documentation. What he says can be accepted as authoritative by both points of view.

Devotees of "other gospels" will find this work a must for their library. For those who have an inquiring mind and are tired of not really knowing, this work will give the answer.

Probably most refreshing of all will be to find out that the author does not presume upon his reader's intelligence. He accepts the premise that he is astute enough to consider the facts and make up his own mind.

As a professional journalist and published author, I find Paul Smith's style fast-paced and easy to read. He writes in a manner that can be understood and appreciated equally well by either the Bible academic or Bible lover.

I recommend this work without reservation. In my opinion, Paul Smith, whom I respect as my Minister and more importantly as my friend, is without doubt Canada's most exciting pulpiteer, author and pacesetter.

DOUGLAS HALL

Toronto, Ontario

CONTENTS

CHAPTER I

IN THE CHAOS OF MODERN RELIGIOUS THOUGHT, WHO IS RIGHT?

Every religion has its own ground rules. Whether they be in the form of a book or tradition or current practice, they constitute the final court of appeal for that particular faith.

Christianity is no exception and before we can determine whether any group can be called Christian or not we must know the ground rules, we must drop some anchors and establish some points of reference. Otherwise, there will be complete chaos.

The Christian Bible is insistent upon the ground rules and the necessity of testing any group of people who call themselves Christians: "Beloved, believe not every spirit, but try the spirits whether they are of God: because many false prophets are gone out into the world. Hereby know ye the Spirit of God: Every spirit that confesseth that Jesus Christ is come in the flesh is of God: And every spirit that confesseth not that Jesus Christ is come in the flesh is not of God: and this is that spirit of anti-christ, whereof ye have heard that it should come; and even now already is it in the world. Ye are of God, little children, and have overcome them: because greater is he that is in you, than he that is in the world. They are of the world: therefore speak they of the world, and the world heareth them. We are of God: he that knoweth God heareth us; he that is not of God heareth not us. Hereby know we the spirit of truth, and the spirit of error" (I John 4: 1-6).

Whatever else this passage says, it indicates that everybody who uses the name of Jesus Christ is not a

Christian. Some of them are quite wrong in their beliefs. The fact that a person is a nice man does not make him right in his religious beliefs. The fact that he belongs to a respectable organization does not mean that he is a Christian. His ability to talk well does not guarantee his Christianity. There are those who are right and there are those who are wrong. How do we tell the difference?

The Religious Headlines of 1967

The chaos of modern religious thought can be seen in the headlines of any daily newspaper. Here is a sample of the headlines that appeared in the Toronto newspapers during the year 1967. Most of these statements were made by ministers of one kind or another, Protestant, Roman Catholic or Jewish, and yet they are the most confusing assemblage of religious ideas imaginable:

January 21—"There is scientific evidence that human beings lived more than one life on this earth."

February 4—"There is no god, the narratives of the Easter resurrection are mythical and must be taken with a 'pinch of salt' and the notion of a life after death is hardly believable."

February 18—"A Catholic priest suggests trial marriage as a cure for divorce."

March 18—"The dropping of the celibacy requirement would be a shameful loss to the church and the world."

April 7—"We Catholics still believe absolutely that the state has no right to grant divorce."

April 15—"Prayer is communion with the inner self."

April 15—"Pre-marital sex should be a matter of free choice."

April 29—"Jesus Christ was a playboy."

May 6—"About a dozen Ontario United Church

ministers speak in tongues."

May 13—"Jesus didn't call men to sit around smoking marijuana."

May 13—"I accept the authority of the Bible and believe in the necessity of personal conversion."

May 20—"A softening in present Catholic thinking on divorce is . . . inevitable."

May 20—"On birth control the pope is going to be damned no matter what his decision is."

May 27—"The basic morality like the law doesn't change."

May 31—"The traditional forms of faith no longer speak vitally to many thinking persons."

June 3—"Unless Christians and Communists draw closer together, they probably will go up in smoke together."

June 10—"Even bishops boost spiritualism in Britain."

June 24—"He claims Jesus didn't die."

June 24—"Minister who takes an occasional puff of marijuana and uses four letter words in conversation."

This is a cross section of the tremendous divergency of opinion that is published constantly leaving the general public with the conclusion that the religious world is in a hopeless state of confusion. Nobody agrees with anybody else. As a result many people conclude that they should have nothing to do with religion at all. Is there any way that we can test statements of this kind to discover whether they represent Christian opinion or not?

Other Religions

I am not concerned about the relative values of Christianity and other religions, such as Islam, Judaism and Hinduism. That is a vitally important topic but it is not our concern in these pages. Our subject should read: "In the Chaos of Modern Religious Thought about Christianity, Who is Right?" Most of us are not concerned about whether we should be Mohammedans or Christians but rather what kind of Christians we should be, or what is a Christian? With so many different opinions, most of them coming from ministers, how do we know what is right?

Terms of Reference

The only possible way of knowing what is right is to have some terms of reference, to have some authority by which we can test the various ideas that we hear. This is true in any field of knowledge. There must be some points of reference or learning stands still. Our ship must be secured to something solid or else it will be at sea. When someone asserts, "Jesus was a playboy", what do we do with it? When another declares, "We ought to change The Ten Commandments", what do we do with that? When a minister says, "There is no life after death". must we accept that? When we read, "There is no such thing as an eternal punishment in hell", what is the test of whether or not this is a Christian concept? Is it just one man's opinion against another's, or are there some terms of reference as far as the Christian faith is concerned?

Rationalism and Opinion

One term of reference that is often suggested is best described by the word "rationalism" or man's ability to think. Our power to think and form opinions is very important. No evangelical should ridicule intelligent inquiry. However, we must recognize the fact that if there is a spiritual world at all, if there is a God, if there is anything beyond animal existence, man's mind does not have the tools with which to deal with it adequately.

This does not mean that our opinions about spiritual things may not be correct but man's opinions are not accepted in any realm until they have been authenticated in some way. Over the years many scientists have had ideas about the causes and cures of certain diseases and sometimes they have been absolutely correct. However, these ideas were of no real value to the people who had these diseases until they were subjected to the scientific terms of reference of experimentation and proof.

In the area of Christianity, I might have a very far-fetched concept about some aspect of heaven and it might be true, but no one is obliged to accept it until it has been lined up with the terms of reference that are acceptable to the Christian faith. Many of the things that we read on the church pages of our newspapers are purely and simply in the realm of personal opinion, not tied to any terms of reference whatsoever. When we get into this realm on spiritual matters, we can come to almost any conclusion.

Tradition

Another group suggests the traditions of the Christian Church as adequate terms of reference. Roman Catholics accept the Bible as the authoritative Word of God but on an equal basis they cling to the traditions of their church. For a Roman Catholic, it is just as important for him to ask the question, "What does the Church say?" as it is to ask, "What does the Bible say?".

Webster's Dictionary defines the word "tradition" in the religious context in this way: "Among Christians, that body of doctrine and discipline, or any article thereof, put forth or revealed by Christ or his apostles, and not committed to writing."[1] For Roman Catholics tradition is just as authoritative and therefore just as significant a term of reference as the written Word of God.

The fact of the matter is that there are some of the traditions of the Roman Catholic Church that just cannot be traced back either to Jesus Christ or the apostles.

In his book, *Faith That Makes Sense*, J. Edwin Orr says: " . . . there is nothing in the Scriptures or the writings of the Fathers of the first three centuries to suggest that the destiny of Mary was different in kind to that of redeemed humanity."[2] Dr. Orr holds a Doctor of Philosophy degree in Religious History from Oxford University and is one of the most prolific writers of our generation.

He is simply stating that in the writings of the early church fathers during the first three centuries, there is no evidence whatever that they thought Mary was any different from any other woman, apart from the fact that she was the mother of Jesus. Every Roman Catholic should know that the doctrine of the Immaculate Conception of Mary "was a subject of long controversy before it finally attained the status of a dogma of the church in the year 1854."[3] This means that it has only been a doctrine of the church for a little more than one hundred years.

At this point, tradition breaks down as a reliable term of reference simply because a great deal of it does not originate where it is supposed to—from Christ and the apostles. Most of it started in a later century.

Roman Catholics know that a tradition would not be accepted if it violated any express teaching of the written Word of God. If we can show a Roman

Catholic that one of his traditional beliefs is contrary to the Scriptures, he is forced to reject it. Tradition, therefore, is not a reliable term of reference because it does not always go back far enough to gain the authority of Jesus and the apostles.

New Revelations

There is another group that relies upon what they feel is a new revelation from God. They reason that we should not be limited to the contents of the Bible which were completed nearly two thousand years ago. Is it not conceivable that God would give us some new revelation? This is the basis of the Mormon Church, the Bible plus a new revelation entitled *The Book of Mormon.* Christian Science is based on the Bible plus a new revelation entitled *Science and Health With Key to the Scriptures.* Spiritualism is based on the Bible plus a continual series of new revelations that come from departed spirits. How can we test these new revelations as far as their authority about the Christian faith is concerned? Are these not a good term of reference?

In his book, *Faith That Makes Sense,* J. Edwin Orr imagines a situation in which the children who have survived World War III emerge from their caves and attempt to reconstruct civilization as their parents had described it to them. They set up some committees—one on law, one on education, one on politics, one on commerce and one on religion.

The first objective of the committee on religion is to see if they can find the sacred writings of the Christian Church. They feel that if they are going to reconstruct the Church they have to find the writings their parents talked about called the Bible. They begin their search. Somebody in Los Angeles finds a book that has the cover burned off but the material in it is obviously a life of Christ. Somebody else in London, England, finds a book with a complete title page, burned a little at the edges but with the print still legible—"New Testament of our Lord and Saviour Jesus Christ."

They find other copies that are exactly the same but in different languages and they add them to their list. Somebody digs up a copy of an Old Testament. Somebody else uncovers a copy of an Old Testament and New Testament combined. Then somebody comes up with an epistle called *The Robe* written by a prophet named Lloyd Douglas. It looks very much like it is part of the sacred Scriptures. Another discovers an epistle called *Science and Health With Key to the Scriptures* written by a prophetess named Mary Baker Eddy. It seems to be a part of the old writings. Still another unearths one called *The Book of Mormon* and it is written by Joseph Smith.

When the committee convened with its collection of books, including *Science and Health, The Book of Mormon, The Robe,* and many other religious books, how would they determine which were actually the sacred Scriptures and which were not? In the first place, they would learn very quickly that nobody ever heard of *The Robe* until the year 1925. *Science and Health* was not in existence until 1875. There was no trace of *The Book of Mormon* until 1825. However, the Christian Church was flourishing long before any of these books came into existence. Therefore, they would automatically discard them simply on the basis of the fact that they did not go back far enough to be identified as original authorities of the Christian Church.[4]

That is precisely the way the Bible was canonized. Every once in a while we hear someone say, "Why accept the Bible as an authority? Don't you realize that it was several hundred years after Christ that the Church finally decided what was to be in the Bible and what was not to be in it?" From this question we are supposed to conclude that the Church made the Bible. The Bible did not make the Church. Therefore, the Church is the supreme authority, not the Bible. However, everybody who knows his religious history is aware of the fact that the Church did not make the Bible; it simply collected those books that had obviously been accepted by the majority of the earliest church fathers right from the very beginning. These were recognized as authentic and the others were not. A study of the church fathers revealed that the entire New Testament had been quoted by them with the exception of eight verses in the Gospel of John. Thus what the church declared to be the Bible several centuries after Christ had been quoted as the Scriptures from the beginning. The church did not suddenly decide that this is the Bible and that is not. It simply canonized the books that the majority of Christians had always accepted as the Bible.

In our generation, if the church had to re-discover the sacred writings, they would do exactly the same thing. They would learn that these new revelations did not have the stamp of authority that took them back to the actual eye-witnesses of Jesus Christ and the apostles and therefore they would not be a valid term of reference for the Christian faith.

The Bible

This brings us to the only authoritative term of reference for the Christian faith—the written Word of God. At this point someone will object: "Look at all the divisions in the Protestant Church and yet they all claim to come from the same Bible."

Actually there are not as many divisions as some

people would like to make out. There are approximately three hundred, some say four hundred, different groups of Protestants, but ninety per cent of these belong to just twenty-four groups. The Methodists and Baptists together in the United States make up 37 million of these.

In most cases, even these are not divided on basic doctrine, but on superficial issues like church government. Should it be democratic or centralized. Or, they are divided on methods of baptism. Should we use a little water or much water. The main body of the traditional creeds that have been historically accepted by the Protestant denominations are almost identical. Why? Because they all come from the same authority—the Bible. There is not as much difference as it would seem on the surface.

Where there is division, it usually comes from one of two sources. It occurs when some other authority than the Bible is accepted, as in the case of Romanism, Mormonism, Christian Science and Spiritualism. It also comes from the difference of opinion among those who doubt the authority of the Bible. This is true in the liberal church. When a man questions the absolute authority of the Scriptures, he can arrive at almost any kind of opinion because he has no absolute terms of reference.

Sir Winston Churchill was not a theologian but he was a very intelligent man cognizant of the world's literature on most subjects. In his book *Thoughts and Adventures* in the chapter called "Moses, the Leader of a People", he says this about the Bible: "We reject, however, with scorn all those learned and laboured myths that Moses was but a legendary figure upon whom the priesthood and the people hung their essential social, moral and religious ordinances. We believe that the most scientific view, the most up-to-date and rationalistic conception, will find its fullest satisfaction in taking the Bible story literally, and in identifying one of the greatest of human beings with the most decisive leap forward ever discernible in the human story . . . In the words of a forgotten work of Mr. Gladstone, we rest with assurance upon 'the impregnable rock of Holy Scripture.'

"Let the men of science and of learning expand their knowledge and probe with their researches every detail of the records which have been preserved to us from these dim ages. All they will do is to fortify the grand simplicity and essential accuracy of the recorded truths which have lighted so far the pilgrimage of man."[5]

Bible Idolatry

If we accept the Bible as our absolute authority, there are those who will accuse us of having made an idol of the Bible. We have idolized a book instead of a person. We are supposed to worship Christ, not a book.

When I was on television with "The coffee house Priest", Malcolm Boyd, I quoted some Scripture and he immediately countered by saying that he was really not very interested in what Jesus said. He was concerned more about what Jesus did. He claimed that he did not idolize a book, he idolized a person.

This sounds very appealing, but where do we find out what Jesus did? If we want to know how Jesus acted, where do we go? There is no other place but the Bible. Contemporary historians dismissed Jesus with a line or two. We can learn almost nothing about Jesus from the historians of His day. Our only source is the Bible.

The Sunday School Curriculum of The United Church of Canada says this: "Well may we wonder what kind of man he (Jesus) was. The only means we have of knowing comes to us from the Bible."[6] Even the extremely liberal United Church Sunday School Curriculum has had to confess that if we want to know anything about Jesus Christ, there is only one authority—the written Word of God which we call the Bible. The opinions we read in the newspapers or the ideas of some of these other forms of faith must be judged by the teaching of the Bible. If they contradict the written Word of God, they are not Christian. There is no other authority. Any intelligent educated person that has even a mediocre knowledge of history is aware of the fact that if he wants the history of Jesus, he must go to the Bible. There is no other source.

What the Bible Teaches

As we discuss these "other gospels", we will insist that their teachings correspond with the Bible. Of course, there will be room for differences in some areas. There are some things that the Bible does not completely clarify. However, on the major doctrines there is little room for variation. If an organization claims to be Christian, then it must be Biblically based on such things as the Deity of Christ, the nature of God, the purpose and destiny of man and the way of salvation. These would be minimum requirements.

It is along these lines, using the written Word of God as our term of reference, that we propose to examine Roman Catholicism, Modernism, Mormonism, Jehovah's Witnesses, Spiritualism, Unitarianism, Christian Science and the most recent to emerge—the Armstrong Polycult.

FOOTNOTES

[1] *Webster's New Collegiate Dictionary* (Toronto: Thomas Allen, 1959), p.901.

[2] J. Edwin Orr, *Faith That Makes Sense* (Valley Forge: Judson Press, 1960), p.59.

[3] J.C. Macaulay, *The Bible and the Roman Church* (Chicago: Moody Press, 1946), pp.69-70.

[4] *Faith That Makes Sense* pp. 67-68.

[5] Winston S. Churchill, *Thoughts and Adventures* (London: MacMillan & Co. Ltd., 1942) pp. 249-250.

[6] James Sutherland Thomson, *God and His Purpose* (Toronto: United Church Publishing House, 1964), p.105.

CHAPTER II

WHAT IS THE ROMAN CATHOLIC WAY
OF SALVATION?

The Roman Catholic Church does not consider any Protestant Church to be a part of the True Church of Jesus Christ. In a little booklet entitled, *What Every Catholic Should Know,* printed in 1954 and bearing the imprimatur of Francis Cardinal Spellman, it is stated this way: "A well-instructed Catholic is convinced that the one true religion is to be found in the Catholic Church—and in this Church only . . . Because Protestant churches do not have these four marks (one, holy, catholic and apostolic), they cannot be recognized as belonging to the true Church of Christ."[1]

Although this was published in a booklet in 1954, the Roman Catholic Church has not changed one iota in this respect. The most recent publication that is being given out today by the Catholic Information Centre in Toronto is a book entitled, *Facts of the Faith*, by Monsignor J. D. Conway. In a dozen different ways, he says exactly the same thing. "We fail to see how any church or denomination which came into existence subsequent to the time of the Apostles, or which has broken the direct line of its descent from them, can claim to be the Church of Christ."[2]

These are by no means isolated examples. This concept, that the visible Roman Catholic Church is indeed the only true church in this world is so much a part of almost every Catholic publication that it is virtually inescapable.

The entire concept of the authority of the Roman Catholic Church being equal to that of the Bible is dependent upon the idea that there is only one visible church—Roman Catholic. For this reason, the one visible church principle must be maintained because on it hangs the authority of some of the basic doctrines of Roman Catholicism. If their doctrines were grounded firmly in the written Word of God, there would be no problem but because a great many of their ideas have no basis whatever in Scripture but only in church tradition, it would cause no end of confusion if they were to drop the one visible church idea.

Mergers are Impossible

Because Roman Catholics do not accept the existence of any other visible true church, there will never be a merger of The Roman Catholic Church and other denominations. How can a church which believes it is the only true visible church on earth merge with another church whose existence is not even admitted?

Catholic dogma absolutely precludes a merger of The Roman Catholic Church with the Anglican, Methodist, Baptist, Presbyterian or any other group. When part of the Anglican Church loses its identity and goes back into the Catholic Church, it will not be a merger or a union. As far as Catholics are concerned, it will be the return of the prodigal.

I can quite well conceive of a day in which Roman Catholics will be willing to drop some of their ideas which are not essential to their basic dogma. There may be changes in the relative power of bishops and Pope. There may be new ideas accepted regarding birth control, but the core of Catholic dogma cannot be altered without violating everything for which they have stood for hundreds of years.

As a result of some of these minor changes, we may live to see the day that the Methodist Church or the Presbyterian Church or the Baptist Church is included in the Roman Catholic Church but in each case it will be a "swallow" not a merger. If this should happen, these other denominations would lose their identity but the Roman Catholic Church would have become stronger than ever.

Protestant Catholic Church

Protestants as well as Roman Catholics have always believed that there is only one Church of Christ on earth. They also believe that that Church is a unity, it is holy, it is universal and it is apostolic. But Protestants believe that it is the invisible body of Christ. No human being acts as its head. That position is reserved for the Lord alone.

We believe that in this invisible Church there are members from almost every visible church in the world. Some of its members are in The United Church of Canada, some in the Roman Catholic Church, some in the Baptist Church, some in The Peoples Church, and others in churches and Christian assemblies throughout the world. Protestants also believe that in all of these visible organizations there are members and adherents who are not a part of the body of Christ at all, members who do not belong to the invisible Church of Jesus Christ.

The questions that concern us in this message are "How does one become a member of the invisible Church of Jesus Christ? How does one become a child of God? What is the way into the body of Christ? How does a man get saved?"

The Way of Salvation

The Protestant answer to these questions might be

summed up in the word "evangelical". Salvation is a result of personal faith in the Lord Jesus Christ at the hearing of the Gospel. The Roman Catholic answer to the same questions could be summed up with the word "sacramental". Salvation is administered by the Roman Catholic Church through the sacraments. There are seven of them—Baptism, Confirmation, the Eucharist, Penance, Extreme Unction, Matrimony and Ordination. The last two, Matrimony and Ordination, are specialized sacraments that are of no concern to us here.

Not a Symbol

We do not properly understand Roman Catholic sacraments unless we realize that they are not mere symbols of spiritual experience. The Roman Church teaches that the sacraments actually produce the results that they signify. In the *Catechism of the Council of Trent for Parish Priests* it says: "They are signs instituted not by man but by God, which we firmly believe have in themselves the power of producing the sacred effects of which they are the signs."[3]

The Council of Trent was called by Pope Paul III in the year 1545 in the Austrian Tyrol. It was the beginning of the Roman Catholic reaction to the Protestant Reformation—a part of the Counter-Reformation. Because it was interrupted by wars, it was not completed until 1563 when Pope Pius IV confirmed its decrees.

Although this took place more than four hundred years ago, modern Roman Catholics still accept it. Fulton Sheen says: "The decrees of the Council of Trent are an official part of Roman Catholic Creed."[4]

The Council of Trent declared that "The faithful must be taught what constitutes a Sacrament. No one can doubt that the sacraments are among the means of attaining righteousness and salvation."[5]

These days we are hearing a great deal about the changes that are taking place in the Roman Catholic Church. When it comes to basic doctrine the literature that is being given out today by Roman Catholics is almost identical in its teaching to the decrees of the Council of Trent. "While the sacraments are signs, they are not mere symbols; they are not mere ceremonies which serve as inspiration. They indicate something which is accomplished in the soul by the very sign itself and by the proper use of that sign. They do not merely show that sanctification has taken place; they accomplish the sanctification and produce it."[6]

Baptism

"Baptism is the Sacrament which makes me a Christian and a member of the Church and gives me the right to receive the other Sacraments . . . The Sacrament of Baptism—1) takes away all sins from my soul, Original Sin, mortal sins and venial sins . . ."[7]

Obviously modern Catholic teaching declares exactly the same thing about Baptism—that it is essential for salvation. Monsignor J. D. Conway puts it this way: "It will help us very much to understand the sacrament of Baptism if we consider the many things it does to our soul.

1. First of all it takes away original sin. That is the significance of the washing—the cleansing action of the water . . .

2. It confers sanctifying grace upon the soul."[8]

Infant Baptism

It is because Catholics believe so firmly that

Baptism is absolutely essential for salvation that they will go to great lengths to make sure that every Catholic baby born in the world is baptized. So important is it that if there is no priest or no member of the Roman Catholic Church to perform the sacrament, anyone can do it so long as he does it correctly and says the right words sincerely.

If a baby has not been baptized, he will never go to heaven. There is no chance for him. "In spite of all the care that we may use, it does occasionally happen that a baby dies without Baptism. What happens to that baby? As far as we can know, it has never received the life of heaven into its little soul, and without the life of heaven it cannot get into heaven. It does not have the capacity or ability to see God or to live in union with God . . . Pope Pius XII summed it up in a talk which he gave to a group of obstetricians on October 29, 1951: 'In the present dispensation there is no other means (except Baptism) of communicating this life (of grace) to the infant who has not yet the use of reason'."[9]

Two of the basic passages Catholics use to confirm the necessity of Baptism for salvation are these: "He that believeth and is baptized shall be saved" (Mark 16:16) and "Except a man be born of water and of the Spirit, he cannot enter into the kingdom of God" (John 3:5).

In the passage from Mark it is quite obvious that the believing is more important than the baptizing because in this discourse the word 'believe' is used five times and the word 'baptize' only once. Whether a person is damned is not connected with his baptism but with his belief: "But he that believeth not shall be damned" (Mark 16:16).

Some commentators doubt whether the phrase 'born of water' in the third chapter of John refers to baptism at all, but even if we grant that it does, no one could possibly read the remainder of Jesus' discourse in this chapter without noticing that baptism as a means of salvation is never mentioned again but being born of the Spirit is repeated three times without any further reference to baptism, and believing as a means of salvation is stressed at least five times. In verse twenty-two of this chapter there is a comparison of John's and Jesus' baptisms, but in neither case are they connected with salvation. However, the chapter ends on this note: "He that believeth on the Son hath everlasting life: and he that believeth not the Son shall not see life; but the wrath of God abideth on him" (John 3:36).

Despite the fact that the New Testament emphasizes trust in Christ far above baptism, Roman Catholic teaching on infant baptism indicates that Catholics stress baptism far above believing. A baby who cannot believe but is baptized will be saved, but a baby who cannot be baptized will be lost. The important thing is not the believing but the baptizing. If the Church of Rome can get a child into heaven despite the fact that he is too young to believe anything, surely it could do exactly the same thing in spite of the fact that it is impossible for a baby to baptize himself. But no, the baby has no hope of ever seeing God without baptism.

It is only fair to say here that Roman Catholic teaching does not condemn babies to hell or even to purgatory simply because they have not been baptized. It says they will go to some place called Limbo where they will be happy but they will never go to heaven.

"It is the traditional belief of Catholic theologians that Almighty God has provided a place of natural happiness for these children who die without

Baptism. For want of a better word, we call the place Limbo. It is a sort of babies' paradise."[10]

Baptism of Desire

"For the adult person who has not had the opportunity of receiving Baptism, there is more reason to hope. He may have the Baptism of desire. This adult person can love God sincerely and honestly, and that love will unite him with God, and when we are united to God in love his grace flows into our soul. Our Lord Jesus Christ has made that very plain."[11]

The Baptism of Desire seems to have been designed originally for people who were actually seeking to become members of the Roman Catholic Church but died before the fact had been accomplished. Now Baptism of Desire seems to have been broadened to include other peoples of the world who are not actually Roman Catholics but have sincerely loved God and lived up to the light they have had. This would include sincere Protestants who through lack of teaching did not know that baptism is necessary for salvation. However, the Baptism of Desire would rule out those Protestants who know all about Roman Catholic teaching on baptism and refuse to rely upon it as a means of salvation.

Baptism of Blood

"The Church teaches that there is another form of Baptism, which she calls the Baptism of Blood. It is martyrdom. It is based on the words of our Lord, 'He who loses his life for my sake, will find it' (Matthew 10:39)."[12]

Confirmation

The sacrament of Confirmation is not considered

essential to salvation but "it is a sin to neglect Confirmation . . . I can get into heaven without Confirmation, but it is more difficult."[1 3]

"For those who have been made Christians by Baptism, still have in some sort the tenderness and softness, as it were, of new-born infants . . . by this Sacrament the Holy Spirit infuses Himself into the souls of the faithful, and increases in them strength and fortitude to enable them, in the spiritual contest, to fight manfully and to resist their most wicked foes."[1 4]

As in the case of Baptism, modern Catholics have not changed their beliefs regarding Confirmation. "Confirmation is like Baptism in that it can be received only once. It makes a spiritual change which is immutable. The soul now bears the mark of a soldier of Christ . . . It gives us particularly the gifts of the Holy Spirit, and it gives us a claim to those special gifts and actual graces which we will need throughout our life in order to bear witness to Christ and lead a holy and fruitful life."[1 5]

Notice that the gifts of the Holy Spirit are dependent upon a sacrament administered by a church and that sacrament is not merely a symbol that this spiritual work has been transacted in a heart but according to Roman Catholic belief, the sacrament itself produces that work.

It would be rather difficult to show that any ritual remotely comparable to Confirmation took place each time the early Christians received the Holy Spirit and His gifts as recorded in the Book of Acts.

The Holy Eucharist

"Catholics believe simply and firmly that when the priest takes bread and wine at Mass, devoutly recalls the scene of the Last Supper, speaks in the name of

Christ and quietly pronounces his sacred words: 'This is my body' and 'This is my blood', that at this very moment Jesus Christ becomes present. The bread and wine are changed into his body and blood, without any change in their appearances. And it is the living Christ who is present there; his human soul is united with his body and blood."[16]

Because some of the elements used in the Eucharist are always kept in a Catholic Church, it is believed that in a very real way Jesus Christ is there. Catholics believe that the bread and the wine are actually the body and blood of the Lord and where they are, He is. This explains why Roman Catholics are so extremely reverent when they are anywhere in the vicinity of their churches. It is also one of the reasons good Catholics attend their churches so frequently. "It is the custom of Catholic people to make frequent visits to the church. It is our Lord's home, and we visit him there as we would any good friend in his home."[17]

Exhortations about the Eucharist are usually based on the sixth chapter of John where Jesus says He is the Bread of Life. This passage is connected directly with the others in the Bible that actually talk about the Eucharist. Of course there is nothing in the Bible that would indicate any necessity for a connection between these passages.

In the fourth chapter of John Jesus compared everlasting life just as definitely to water when He was talking to the woman of Samaria. It is a little difficult to understand why this passage should be interpreted as spiritual water only and the passage about bread should be interpreted both spiritually and materially.

Using the sixth chapter of John, the Parish Priest is urged to tell the people that spiritual life is dependent upon partaking of the Eucharist and that in some way the resurrection of the just is connected with it. However, the main point seems to be a means of bringing the living Christ into actual contact with the believer.

Penance

More than four hundred years ago the Council of Trent declared: "For those who fall into sin after Baptism the Sacrament of Penance is as necessary to salvation as is Baptism for those who have not been already baptized . . . As he who suffers shipwreck has no hope of safety, unless, perchance, he seize on some plank from the wreck, so he that suffers the shipwreck of baptismal innocence, unless he cling to the saving plank of Penance, has doubtless lost all hope of salvation." [18]

Catholics today believe exactly the same thing about Penance: "Here are some of the things the sacrament of Penance does for our souls:

1. It restores sanctifying grace, if we have lost it by mortal sin. In other words, it revives supernatural life in our souls when we have killed that life by separating ourselves from God's love, . . .

5. The external punishments of hell are taken away. If we should die without sanctifying grace, we would never be capable of getting into heaven, and hell would be the only place available to us. If we should die as enemies of God, we would remain his enemies forever, separated from him, excluded from his home." [19]

Although some Roman Catholic publications state that the sacrament of baptism is the only one that is necessary for salvation, it is impossible to read the teaching about Penance without concluding that where mortal sin is involved it is just as necessary for salvation as baptism. Without it, the soul goes to hell. With it, the soul is saved from "the eternal punishments of hell."

Penance involves three things on the part of the person who has sinned—contrition, confession and satisfaction. Satisfaction usually involves doing some acts of service, worship or prayer that the priest suggests. It does two things: 1) It eliminates some of the temporal punishment that might be involved, and 2) It gives the soul additional strength to face the future.

The priest does two things in the sacrament of Penance. He suggests the proper 'satisfaction' and he absolves the sin. The actual words that the priest says in Latin are these: "May our Lord Jesus Christ absolve you, and I by His authority do absolve you from any bond of excommunication or interdict, insofar as I am able and you have need of it. Then I absolve you from all your sins in the name of the Father and of the Son and of the Holy Spirit. Amen."[20]

Extreme Unction

"Extreme Unction is the culminating sacrament. All of life is a preparation for death, and it has now reached its final step. Ahead is eternity."[21]

The final Roman Catholic sacrament is based on a passage in the Book of James: "Is any sick among you? Let him call for the elders of the church; and let them pray over him, anointing him with oil in the name of the Lord: And the prayer of faith shall save the sick, and the Lord shall raise him up; and if he have committed sins, they shall be forgiven him." (James 5:14-15).

Even a casual comparison of this passage and the sacrament of Extreme Unction would raise some questions. How was the transition made from a simple prayer for the recovery of the sick to the rather complicated sacrament designed to carry a sick person through death and into the next life? Or, how did a group of elders become changed into a single priest? At this point the Roman Catholic Church is forced to seek refuge in the arms of its tradition because the written Word of God simply does not support the sacrament of Extreme Unction.

In this sacrament the priest "gently traces the sign of the Cross on the sick person's eyes, ears, nose, mouth, hands, and feet. While he is anointing the eyes he says, in Latin: 'By this holy anointing and by this kindness and mercy, may our Lord forgive you whatever sins you have committed by sight.' Similar words are said for the other anointings, asking God to forgive the sins of hearing, smelling, taste and speech, touch and walking—the sins we have walked into."[2] [2]

Punishment

Now that we have discussed the five sacraments that have to do with all Roman Catholics, we might well ask the question, What are the results?

The Catholic who has observed all of the sacraments faithfully is saved from eternal punishment for his sins. There is no real assurance of salvation because it is rather difficult to be absolutely certain that one has been successful in making his way down this complicated Roman Catholic road.

Even if the believer has been saved from eternal punishment, he is still subject to temporal punishment for his sins. This may take place in several different ways. There could be direct acts of God which punish him here and now or he can go to Confession and volunteer to do the penance that is required. The remainder of his temporal punishment is carried out in Purgatory. The Roman Catholic Church is able to give very little information about who is in Purgatory or how long they may have to stay there. "The Church has no control over purgatory or the souls who are there. She does not even claim to know which souls are there or how long they may need to stay."[2][3]

The Roman Catholic goes through his life and if he is a good man he works very hard and sincerely at his religion. He attends church faithfully and frequently but he is never really sure that he has 'made it' until after he dies. The best he can say is "I hope so."

Conclusion

The Bible says: "For God so loved the world, that he gave his only begotten Son, that whosoever believeth in him should not perish, but have everlasting life" (John 3:16).

Between "believeth in him" and "have everlasting life" the Roman Catholic Church has arbitrarily inserted the sacraments of Baptism, Confirmation, Eucharist, Penance and Extreme Unction and after that leaves its members dangling in the uncertainty of a purgatory that is never mentioned once in the Bible.

The Bible says: "As many as received him, to them gave he power to become the sons of God, even to them that believe on his name" (John 1:12). Between "received him" and "become the sons of God" the Roman Catholic Church has arbitrarily inserted the ritual of a religion, much of which cannot be found in the Bible at all.

The Roman Catholic Church declares that the way to God is the church, the priest, Mary, Joseph, the sacraments, purgatory. Jesus said: "I am the way, the truth, and the life: no man cometh unto the Father, but by me" (John 14:6).

FOOTNOTES

[1] *What Every Catholic Should Know* (Montreal: Palm Publishers, 1955), pp. 7 and 9.

[2] John Donald Conway, *Facts of the Faith* (New York: All Saints Press, 1961), p. 107.

[3] *Catechism of the Council of Trent for Parish Priests* (Translated by John A. McHugh and Charles J. Callan, New York: Joseph F. Wagner, Inc., 1923), p. 146.

[4] *World Book Encyclopedia* (Chicago: Field Enterprises Educational Corp., 1962), Vol. 17, p. 352.

[5] *Catechism of the Council of Trent for Parish Priests* p. 143.

[6] Conway, *Facts of the Faith*, p. 129.

[7] William J. Cogan, *A Catechism for Adults* (Chicago: ACTA Publications, 1951), p. 55.

[8] Conway, *Facts of the Faith*, p. 139.

[9] Ibid., pp. 142 and 143.

[10] Ibid., p. 143.

[11] Ibid.

[12] Ibid., p. 144

[13] Cogan, *A Catechism for Adults,* p. 58.

[14] *Catechism of the Council of Trent for Parish Priests*, pp. 209 and 211.

[15] Conway, *Facts of the Faith,* pp. 152 and 153.

[16] Ibid., p. 154.

[17] Ibid., p. 162.

[18] *Catechism of the Council of Trent for Parish Priests*, p. 261.

[19] Conway, *Facts of the Faith,* pp. 193 and 194.

[20] Ibid., p. 217.

[21] Ibid., p. 228.

[22] Ibid., p. 230.

[23] Ibid., p. 221.

CHAPTER III

WHAT ARE THE BLUNDERS OF MODERNISM?

Modernism is the greatest single threat to the Christian faith today. It is much more devastating than any of the other groups that we sometimes refer to as False Cults. Even the largest of these influences only a few thousand people, whereas liberal theology has had an effect on the entire organized church. Only a few of the new smaller denominations are completely free of it. It starts with the theologians, moves into the seminaries and gradually filters through to the people. As a result, millions of men and women that have had some kind of Christian background have either adopted a liberal position themselves or, more often, have abandoned the church.

The Road to Atheism

Liberal theologians have started the organized churches down a pathway that can lead only to atheism. The first step is taken when a man chooses to doubt the inerrancy and absolute authority of the Bible. Of course, every intelligent person is aware of the fact that there are many problems in the Bible and we do not have the solution to all of them. When a man becomes cognizant of these problems for the first time, there is a choice that lies before him:

He may decide that the problems are so serious he can no longer accept the Bible completely and he leaves room for inaccuracies, mythology, scientific blunders and historical mistakes. Or he may choose to accept the Bible with its problems and conclude that there is a satisfactory solution to every one of them despite the fact that he himself may not know it.

It is vitally important to remember that at this point a choice is involved. It is not a question of whether we will accept the accuracy and authority of the Bible despite concrete, scientific proof to the contrary or that we will reject the authority of the Bible despite concrete, scientific proof that it is the Word of God. As a matter of fact, neither is the case. There is no final evidence that can prove the validity of either position. It remains a matter of faith and it depends upon the choice that we make on the basis of the evidence.

Many years ago two promising young preachers were asked to speak at the Forest Home Christian Conference in the mountains of California. Both were at the age when they were becoming aware of some of the difficult problems in the Bible. Both read everything they could find on the subject. They were both intelligent people. One decided in favour of doubt and he began to question seriously the authenticity and accuracy of some portions of Scripture. The other decided in favour of faith—he resolved that he would accept the Bible with its problems as the inerrant and authoritative Word of God. The name of the first young man was Charles B. Templeton. Today he is out of the ministry. The name of the second was Billy Graham. The effect of his worldwide ministry will undoubtedly be a part of the religious history of this generation.

"God-is-Love-Only"

Once a man leaves room for inaccuracy in the Bible, he can adopt the "God-is-Love-and-Nothing-Else" theology. This is the outlook of the average liberal and it depends upon a doubtful view of inspiration. The only way that anyone could think of God as a God of Love *only* would be to treat lightly or with complete indifference those passages in the Scriptures that stress the holiness and justice and vengance of God. The modernist cannot conceive of a God who would destroy people because of their sin or a God who would choose to judge a nation by having another nation declare war on it. Of course the Bible has many examples of this sort of thing, both in the Old and New Testaments, and the liberal theologian simply refuses to accept them as a part of the infallible Word of God.

Actually this over-emphasis on the love of God does not solve the problem of human suffering anyway. The modernist is still left with a God who has permitted the tragedies of the world to go on without intervening. The Bible describes a God who is in supreme command. Certainly He is pictured as a God of Love who is merciful, gracious and long-suffering but He is also pictured as a God of absolute holiness and justice and, although we may not always know why God permits suffering and sometimes punishes an entire nation with severe judgment, we are willing to conclude that God does know what He is doing and it is for the best.

In liberal theology, the "God-is-love-and-nothing-else" god apparently concerns himself with other things and stands passively by while men destroy each other.

In this dilemma the honest liberal throws up his hands in despair and either adopts a position of "Christian agnosticism" or follows his theology to its logical conclusion—atheism. However, in our generation atheism has been adorned with a new description—"God is Dead".

Are Liberals Christians?

It is impossible for any person to say unequivocally that another man is or is not a Christian. Certainly we can assess a set of beliefs, we can read a book, but only God knows the heart. I suspect that a number of modernists have had an experience with Jesus Christ early in life and that their anti-Biblical ideas have penetrated no farther than their heads.

Perhaps one of the most outspoken leftwing ministers in our immediate vicinity is The Reverend Ernest Marshall Howse who was the bombastic Moderator of The United Church of Canada in the mid-sixties. Dr. Howse has made a great many extreme statements which have been quoted in the press from coast to coast. Some of his ideas are so "far out" that a group of the theological students in Immanuel College—The United Church seminary—wrote to him and strenuously objected.[1]

It has been my privilege to meet Dr. Howse personally and to share some correspondence with him. My heart was warmed by the final paragraph of a personal letter that he wrote to me dated December 30, 1966: "I am sure that people who are radically different in Biblical scholarship, and in theological belief, can be equally committed to Jesus Christ as spiritual Master and Lord."

The Danger

The devastating effects of an anemic view of inspiration which will admit errors and contradictions in the Bible is generally not to be found in the first generation but in the children and the students of that generation. Most of the modernists with whom we are familiar started their lives with both an authoritative Bible and a God. Somewhere along the line they may have lost their Bible but they have managed to retain their God. However, the next generation will start *without* an authoritative Bible but at least some conception of God. With this insecure foundation, it will not be long before they lose both their Bible and their God.

One of the most shocking results of modernism and its effect upon the second generation can already be seen in the appalling dearth of ministerial students in the liberal denominations. Churches of this kind just do not produce sufficient volunteers for the ministry to fill their own pulpits and quite often the students they do have come from evangelical churches.

Anti-Intellectualism

Liberals are fond of accusing evangelicals of anti-intellectualism but modernism has developed its own brand of anti-intellectualism. It can be seen in at least two areas—a lack of honesty in presenting the facts and a tendency toward an absolutely closed mind.

Honesty

On Sunday afternoon, September 3, 1967, Billy Graham preached to some 45,000 people at the grandstand of the Canadian National Exhibition—the largest crowd ever to be assembled at this place for any reason. The following week a story appeared in the *Toronto Daily Star* under the caption, "Evangelical spectacular", by Ron Evans. Mr. Evans is a newspaper reporter but what he had to say reflects the thought of modernistic ministers who strive desperately to find fault with Billy Graham's crusades.

"The one aspect of his address I found most

remarkable, however, was his apparent scorn of education and 'intellect'. Again and again, the words 'intellectual', 'intellectualizing', and 'intellectualism' kept cropping up, and always, it seemed linked with disbelief, if not downright evil. For instance, '. . . educated, intellectual monsters like Goebbels, with his PHD . . .' and '. . . Stalin's daughter, reared in atheism and an intellectual . . .'."[2]

If he was not already aware of it, a simple inquiry would have revealed the fact that there are at least two men on the Billy Graham Team that hold Ph.D. degrees from major universities and that one of them in the person of Dr. John Wesley White was sitting on the platform that very afternoon. White holds a doctorate from Oxford University.

If he had inquired a little further, he would have learned that in the Berlin Congress which was convened by Billy Graham in 1966, another Star reporter had actually counted more than one hundred Ph.D.'s.[3]

Apart from these facts, any twelve year old who had listened to Billy Graham's sermon would have understood what he was saying—that intellectual achievement will not get a man to God. He used Goebbels as an illustration of the fact that a Ph.D. will not keep a man from being bad. He referred to Stalin's daughter to show that an intellectual can be an atheist.

It is obvious then that Ron Evans was either ignorant of the facts or was dishonest in their presentation.

Misquotes

In "Voice of the People", a feature of the *Vancouver Province,* there was a letter to the editor under the caption "We can get along without Bible salvation."[4] It was written by Rev. Jim McKibbon of St. Anselm's Anglican Church in Vancouver. Apparently Mr. McKibbon hasn't much time for either Billy Graham or Paul Smith—certainly he has no use for our theology. After taking Billy Graham to task because he chose to say nothing about the war in Vietnam, this Anglican minister proceeded to quote a number of things about me that he had read in the *Toronto Daily Star* of August 26, 1967: "He acknowledged that there were 12 men in his congregation who committed adultery but said he would not hire a rehabilitated criminal to work in his garden."

I suppose Mr. McKibbon was trying to demonstrate how inconsistent a fundamentalist can be by suggesting that I would permit men in my congregation who had committed adultery but would not let a rehabilitated criminal cut the grass in my backyard. And he would have been quite right in his accusation. However, it would seem that this Anglican Liberal cannot read or else he lacks the honesty to quote what he does read accurately.

The article to which Mr. McKibbon referred was written by Allen Spraggett, the Religious Editor of the *Toronto Daily Star* and it appeared on August 26 under the caption "Religious razzle dazzle." Mr. Spraggett quoted me quite accurately as making the following statements in several different sermons on a variety of topics:

1. "There are at least 12 men in this congregation who have committed adultery—on the basis of the law of averages" (on Morality).

2. "I'm sure no one here would hire the rehabilitated murder-rapist as his gardener to work where his little daughter is playing" (on Capital Punishment).

After this appalling demonstration of dishonesty, Rev. Jim McKibbon of St. Anselm's Anglican Church, Vancouver concluded his letter by saying, "If this is 'Bible salvation' we can do without it—thank you just the same."

Anyone who knows the facts would have to say, "If this is modernism, it is a menace to the intellect of modern man."

"Through gothic windows"

Another example of the same sort of dishonesty that is common to liberal theologians is to be found in a piece written by E. Gilmour Smith in *The United Church Observer* entitled "Through gothic windows." The subject in this case happened to be Bob Jones University—one of the most remarkable schools to be found anywhere in the world today.

After saying several rather stupid things about the university, Dr. Smith says, "The university has attracted an enrolment of 3,500 drawn mostly from Hard-shell Baptists, the Holy Rollers, and similar groups."[5]

If the author had been willing to spend a few minutes in any good religious library, he would have discovered that Hard-shell Baptists are a very small group in the United States who numbered only 69,000 back in the 1950's and they are particularly noted for their hyper-calvinism.[6] On the other hand, the term "Holy Rollers" does not designate any particular group but is used as a form of ridicule for any Christians who are overly emotional in their religious response. These people are known for their hyper-arminianism.[7] It is rather obvious that the same university would not attract people who are poles apart on a single doctrine.

An additional five minutes in the library would

have revealed that the Hard-shell Baptists do not believe in Sunday Schools or Missionary Societies and yet there are more than thirty different denominational Sunday Schools in Bob Jones University as well as a great many missionary societies among the students.

I attended Bob Jones University for two years when it was located in Cleveland, Tennessee. Both years when I was there one of these highly emotional groups held a mammoth convention not far from the university campus. As a matter of fact, it was so close that on a still night we could hear their singing coming through our dormitory windows. However, the faculty and administration of the school was so much opposed to this sort of thing that the students were not permitted to attend any of the convention meetings without suffering a severe penalty.

The fact of the matter is that the student body of Bob Jones University has very few, if any, who could be classified as either "Holy Rollers" or Hard-shell Baptists. The overwhelming majority would consist of Baptists from the major Baptist denominations, Presbyterians, Methodists, Lutherans, Episcopalians, Congregationalists, etc.

The only conclusion to which we can come then is that the author of this piece is either ignorant of the facts or else he lacks the honesty to state them. If his problem is ignorance then of course he should not be writing articles for *The United Church Observer.* If, on the other hand, he is deliberately being dishonest with the facts, he constitutes a serious menace to intellectualism.

This particular author usually tends to write about science—the age of the rocks, the story they tell, the dinosaurs that lived on this earth long ago, and so on. If a minister cannot state the facts honestly when he writes about a Christian university which he is in a position to know something about, how can we expect him to be reliable when he begins to meddle in the scientific field which he knows very little about.

The Closed Mind

Another area in which the anti-intellectualism of the modernist can be seen is in his tendency toward an absolutely closed mind. In his beautifully written volume on The Old Testament, Dr. Ernest Marshall Howse says: "The Bible, we may put it briefly, is a book dealing with an historical reality—man's search after God ... The Bible is the record of how men came up from the crude, the base, and the revolting to the truth as it is in Jesus."[8]

This sort of statement that depicts man climbing from "the crude. the base, and the revolting" to his present position is a little hard to swallow if one has just read the two consecutive issues of *Life* magazine which tell the unbelievably ugly story of syndicated crime in North America.[9]

Dr. Howse then proceeds to express his attitude toward others who might approach the Bible as a literal revelation of God: "Once one has awakened to appreciation of the real nature, scope and purpose of the Scriptures, all such distortion (literalistic) of the Bible appears for what it is: unadulterated nonsense, unworthy of the consideration of an intelligent Bible student."[10] (Parenthesis mine.)

This seems to be a rather blunt way of saying, "Anyone who doesn't agree with me at this point is not worth considering."

There are a great many able scholars who would not agree with Dr. Howse for a moment in his thesis that The Old Testament is the story of man's search after God. It would be difficult to spend time in the most elementary seminary course on The Old Testament without running into the work of C.F. Keil, the German scholar.

In the *Biblical Commentary on The Old Testament* which he co-authored with F. Delitzsch, he says this: "The Holy Scriptures of the Old Testament contain the divine revelations which prepared the way for the redemption of fallen man by Christ."[11]

The modernist puts on intellectual blinders and refuses to consider any opinion but his own. Another word for such a person is a bigot.

Two of the basic prerequisites of intellectual pursuit in any field of knowledge are absolute honesty and an open mind. Anyone who is dishonest with the facts and has a closed mind is guilty of anti-intellectualism.

Social Problems

Modernism attempts to deal with social problems on the surface—where it is sometimes easier—instead of getting to the heart of the problem—where it is usually difficult.

Jesus established the priority of the Gospel when He answered the lawyer's question, "Master, which is the great commandment in the law? Jesus said unto him, Thou shalt love the Lord thy God with all thy heart, and with all thy soul, and with all thy mind. This is the first and great commandment. And the second is like unto it, Thou shalt love thy neighbour as thyself" (Matthew 22:36-39).

A man's relationship to God comes first and his obligation to his neighbour second. Modernists have a tendency to concentrate only on the second and pass very lightly over the first. This is the easy and sometimes irresponsible way out.

It is quite possible for a man to be involved in

some remote social causes and fail utterly to be a real
Christian where he lives. It may have been easier for
some clergymen to leave Detroit and join the march
to Selma than to stay and deal with the problems in
Detroit that caused a riot much worse than Alabama
has ever seen. Both should be done by Christian
people but they will be done as a result of men whose
hearts have been changed by the power of God—not
men who have adopted a do-good-away-from-home
philosophy.

It is much easier to protest the morality of the war
in Vietnam than it is to deal with the conflict that
sometimes rages in your own home and your marriage
relationship. The first requires only a crusading spirit.
The second necessitates a changed life.

It is not too difficult to write thousands of words
about poverty and housing, but it is a most difficult
thing to accept a Gospel that demands a right about
turn in my personal life. Once again both are
necessary but we should remember that these men
who wage war on their typewriters against social evils
sometimes act like the devil personally while they are
writing like a saint publicly.

Many people are willing to climb on the
bandwagon of the social Gospel because they protest
the implications of the whole Gospel of Christ which
intrudes on their privacy and insists that they change
their way of living.

The liberal churches are issuing a great many
statements these days about their concern for the
social problems of our civilization. A few days ago a
Toronto newspaper carried this item: "The National
Council of Church's general board adopted a
sweeping civil rights program . . .

"The program included: A reverse economic
boycott on businesses that practise discrimination . . .

Commit 10 per cent of the national council's budget to 'high-risk, low-return' investments in the nation's ghettoes . . ."[12] This is commendable, to say the least, but the tragedy of a pronouncement such as this is that these representatives of the Christian churches have not said one word about the primary problem—the crying need of both Whites and Blacks to have a personal relationship with God through Jesus Christ.

The problem is really one of priority—a problem with which Jesus was confronted many times. As a matter of fact this was His major criticism of the religious organizations of His day—not that they were doing bad things but that they had lost their sense of Scriptural priority.

"Woe unto you, scribes and Pharisees, hypocrites! for ye pay tithe of mint and anise and cummin, and have omitted the weightier matters of the law, judgment, mercy, and faith: these ought ye to have done, and not to leave the other undone. Ye blind guides, which strain at a gnat, and swallow a camel."

Our liberal friends would immediately pounce on the words judgment and mercy to prove that in this passage Jesus is saying that social responsibility is more important than religious observances. With this we would heartily concur but the priority of the Gospel is established in the next two verses where Jesus describes the most effective way to produce judgment, mercy and faith.

"Woe unto you, scribes and Pharisees, hypocrites! for ye make clean the outside of the cup and of the platter, but within they are full of extortion and excess. Thou blind Pharisee, cleanse first that which is within the cup and platter, that the outside of them may be clean also" (Matthew 23:23-26).

Justice, mercy and faith are very definitely more

important than gifts of money to the church but
these "weightier matters of the law" can be produced
only by a change of heart. This is the *primary*
purpose of the Gospel of Jesus Christ.

Mops and Buckets

Not long ago I went into my basement one
morning and discovered the entire floor covered with
water after a rather heavy rain. Immediately we got
some mops and buckets and began cleaning up the
mess. However, my main concern was to find where
the water was coming in. I realized that unless I was
able to stop the water at its source, we might go on
using our mops and buckets indefinitely and never
accomplish our purpose. Needless to say, the source
was found and stopped.

The modernist is doing a fine job with his bucket
and his mop but he has made the tragic blunder of
concentrating all of his attention on the "mess" in
the world and has given little, if any, attention to its
cause.

Certainly the mopping up needs to be done but we
should not have left the other undone.

FOOTNOTES

[1] Allen Spraggett, "The Theology Students Versus
Dr. Ernest Howse", *The Toronto Daily Star*, May 14,
1966, p. 63.

[2] Ron Evans, "Evangelical Spectacular", *The
Toronto Daily Star*, Sep. 5, 1967, p. 43.

[3] Allen Spraggett, "Evangelical Christianity", *The
Toronto Daily Star* Nov. 5, 1966, p. 65.

[4] Jim McKibbon, "We Can Get Along Without
Bible Salvation", *The Vancouver Province*, Sep. 9,
1967, p. 4.

[5] E. Gilmour Smith, "Through Gothic Windows", *The United Church Observer,* Vol. CXXXVII, No. 7 and Vol. XXVIII, No. 22, Feb. 15, 1967, p. 39.

[6] Robert G. Torbet, "Hard-Shell Baptists", *Twentieth Century Encyclopedia of Religious Knowledge* (Grand Rapids: Baker Book House, 1955), Vol. I, p. 490.

[7] Elmer T. Clark, Ibid., p. 523.

[8] Ernest Marshall Howse, *The Lively Oracles* (London: George Allen and Unwin Ltd., 1956), p. 14.

[9] *Life Magazine,* Sep. 1, 1967, Vol. 63, No. 9, p. 15 and Sep. 8, 1967, Vol. 63, No. 10, p. 91, "The Mob".

[10] Howse, *The Lively Oracles,* p. 17.

[11] C.F. Keil, *Biblical Commentary on the Old Testament* (Grand Rapids: Wm. B. Eerdmans), Vol. 1, p. 9.

[12] "Churchmen blame whites for U.S. race rioting", *The Toronto Daily Star,* Sep. 15, 1967, p. 29.

CHAPTER IV

WHO ARE THE MORMONS AND WHAT DO THEY TEACH?

Mormonism could prove to be one of the best counterfeits of historical Christianity that will ever be devised by man. It uses exactly the same terminology that has been common to the Christian Church throughout its history and it claims to be based on a belief in the authority of the Bible. An innocent Christian could talk with a Mormon missionary many times without realizing the great gulf that exists between Mormon teaching and the Bible.

The Mormon Church has more than two million members in the world today—the majority of them in the United States. Their compulsory tithing nets an annual income in excess of $110,000,000. They have thirteen thousand missionaries throughout the world who support themselves, and their work is so successful that they are able to build an average of three hundred new chapels every year.[1] They claimed 90,000 baptisms throughout the world in 1961,[2] and they can boast more adherents in *Who's Who in America* than any other single denomination.[3]

The Great Apostasy

The standard authoritative works of the Mormon Church include four books—*The Bible, The Book of Mormon, The Doctrine and Covenants* and *The Pearl of Great Price.* Mormons believe that all other Christian groups have been in a state of apostasy for hundreds of years and that their church constitutes the "restoration"·of the original. Their first prophet,

Joseph Smith, set the pace for all of their people in *The Pearl of Great Price.* "My object in going to inquire of the Lord was to know which of all the sects was right, that I might know which to join . . .

"I was answered that I must join none of them, for they were all wrong; and the Personage who addressed me said that all their creeds were an abomination in his sight; that those professors were all corrupt."[4]

It is interesting to note that during this period when Joseph Smith decided that all the churches were in an apostate condition they were in fact going through one of the greatest periods of revival in church history. This was the era of Charles G. Finney and D.L. Moody who, along with many other great leaders, profoundly affected the destiny of the Christian Church. Immediately following the ministry of Moody came the Welch revival which once again was reminiscent of the Acts of the Apostles. It would seem that the First Prophet of the Mormon Church was completely ignorant of these movements which of course are now simple facts of history.

Modern Mormon missionaries start with Joseph Smith's declaration of universal apostasy and it is not difficult to convince the average Christian that because of the many divisions in the Church something must be wrong. Mormons are quick to point out that there are hundreds of different kinds of Protestant Christians and the very existence of these proves the inadequacy of the Bible and the need of some more complete revelation to explain the real meaning of the Bible.

Gordon B. Hinckley, one of the modern exponents of Mormonism, puts it this way: "They regard it (the Bible) as not being complete as a guide. Scores of different types of church organization and conflicting interpretations on basic doctrines, which have led to the creation of hundreds of different sects, bear witness to the inadequacy of the Bible."[5] (Parenthesis mine.)

What is the Answer?

The informed Christian should be able to counter this argument on two levels. In the first place, it is not difficult to prove that even the visible Church is not as divided as her enemies would like to make out. For instance, in 1961 the Dominion Bureau of Statistics in Canada reported that the total population was 18,238,247. Buddhists, Confucianists, Jews and Catholics accounted for 9,043,313. Extremely small religious groups and those who had no religion at all accounted for 415,062. The overwhelming bulk of the Protestants— 8,779,872—were accounted for in only seventeen different denominational groups. More than eight million of these people declared themselves to be members of only five different churches—United, Anglican, Presbyterian, Baptist and Lutheran.[6] This means that 92.8% of all the Protestants in Canada can be found in just five groups. Each of these five denominations would accept the *Apostles Creed* as a good statement of their basic beliefs throughout their history. Any informed person is quite aware of the fact that the differences between the major denominations have not centered around the basic doctrines. This was even more evident when Joseph Smith lived than it is today because at that time liberalism had not made any serious inroads.

In the second place, Mormons fail to realize that The Church is not made up of denominations and organizations but rather it is a group of people who have come to know Jesus Christ as their Saviour and

Lord. This kind of person can be found in almost every denomination. Unfortunately, it would be difficult to find any Christian organization that did not have among its membership both Christians and non-Christians—people who were saved and people who were unsaved. However, in any gathering of real Christians it is soon apparent that they all believe virtually the same basic truths. It would be an interesting experience for a Mormon to attend a luncheon of the Christian Business Men's Committees or a camp meeting of the Gideons or a Youth for Christ rally or an Inter-Varsity Christian Fellowship where he would find representatives from many different denominations but bound together by the basic common denominators of their faith found in the Bible.

The fact of the matter is that there has been no apostasy of The Church of Jesus Christ. It has been in existence for nearly two thousand years. It always has been and still is united and, therefore, there is no need for a "Restoration."

In the short period of 137 years, the Mormon Church has suffered a number of splits. According to one authority who was converted from Mormonism, there are at least thirty different Mormon sects. He lists six of them: The Church of Jesus Christ of Latter-day Saints, The Reorganized Church of Jesus Christ of Latter-day Saints, Church of Christ (Temple Lot), Church of Jesus Christ (Bickertonites), Church of Jesus Christ (Cutlerites), and Church of Jesus Christ (Strangites).[7]

The Book of Mormon

The fantastic story of the origin of *The Book of Mormon* can be found in detail in any copy of the book written as a sort of preface or introduction to the actual contents. It claims to be a miraculous translation from an unknown language—Reformed Egyptian—made by Joseph Smith from golden plates that he found in the ground. Since the plates themselves were taken back by an angelic messenger after the translation had been made, it was necessary to have witnesses to the fact that Joseph Smith's story about them was true. Thus in every *Book of Mormon* there is the testimony first of three witnesses and then eight to the validity of the story.

The Three Witnesses

One of the many embarrassing things to Mormons about their own history is the fact that all three of these witnesses became apostates to the Mormon Church and were soundly denounced by their Mormon brethren. Two of them were re-baptized into the church at a later date, and one, Martin Harris, completely changed his statement. "I did not see them (the golden plates) as I do that pencil case, yet I saw them with the eye of faith. I saw them just as distinctly as I saw anything about me—though at the time they were covered over with a cloth."[8] (Parenthesis mine.)

The Eight Witnesses

The testimony of the eight witnesses loses a great deal of its effectiveness when one realizes that four of them were Whitmers, the fifth was married to a Whitmer, the sixth was Joseph Smith's father and the last two were his brothers, Hyrum and Samuel.

The King James Version

The story of *The Book of Mormon* covers a period of history from 600 B.C. to 421 A.D. The golden plates in the original Reformed Egyptian were supposed to have been buried at the end of this period and they were not translated by Joseph Smith until 1830. Despite these facts, it contains scores of quotations directly from the King James Version of the Bible—at least twenty-seven thousand words.[9] This version of the Bible did not appear until 1611—1,190 years after the plates were buried and 219 years before Joseph Smith made his translation. It is difficult to understand why the English of King. James is used when it was totally unknown to the people who wrote the originals and was certainly not used by Joseph Smith and his contemporaries.

The obvious answer would seem to be that much of *The Book of Mormon* is copied directly from the King James Version of the Bible.

This becomes an even more embarrassing problem for the Mormons when they realize that Joseph Smith naively copied the mistakes of the King James Version as well as its language. "The Father, and the Son, and the Holy Ghost are one."[10] The only place in the Bible where the doctrine of the Trinity is supported by a direct statement is The First Epistle of John. "For there are three that bear record in heaven, the Father, the Word, and the Holy Ghost: and these three are one" (5:7). Apparently, Joseph Smith copied this from the King James Version not knowing that this verse does not appear in any of the ancient manuscripts of the New Testament and Biblical scholars universally agree that it was added at a later date. Although there are many other passages that leave no room for doubt as to the validity of the doctrine of the Trinity, this is not one of them.

"And whoso believeth in me, and is baptized, the same shall be saved . . . And whoso believeth not in me, and is not baptized, shall be damned."[11] This, of course, is a quotation from the Gospel of Mark where

Jesus said: "He that believeth and is baptized shall be saved; but he that believeth not shall be damned" (16:16). Once again, this passage is not to be found in the ancient manuscripts and most Bible scholars believe it was added at a later date. This fact has now been noted in most of the modern versions of the Bible but Joseph Smith's "divinely revealed" translation of the golden plates leaves this doubtful passage intact.

The Story is Unreliable

"The Book of Mormon gives a very definite account of who the American Indians are and how they came to the western hemisphere."[1] [2]

The author attempts to confirm the validity of Smith's story by saying: "Modern archeological research has accounted for many of these buried cities; uncovered cement highways mentioned in the Book of Mormon; located temples and other magnificent buildings erected by those people who reached a high stage of civilization and culture in the land of America."[1] [3]

Unfortunately for the Mormon cause this statement about modern archeology is not documented in any form by the author. This opinion is not attributed to any accepted authority on the subject. As a matter of fact, there is a considerable amount of documented material that contradicts the story of *The Book of Mormon*. One of the men who has done vast research on Mormonism is Rev. R. Odell Brown, pastor of the Hillcrest Methodist Church, Fredericksburg, Virginia. Dr. Brown wrote to the Department of Anthropology at Columbia University in New York City and received an answer which included this statement. "I do not believe that there is a single thing of value concerning the pre-history of the

Holy Ghost, and bring forth a son, yea, even the Son of God."[23]

Plagiarism

Many authorities who have spent a great deal of time with the original documents concerning *The Book of Mormon* are suspicious that the historical part of the book was copied directly from a manuscript by Solomon Spaulding. One of the many people who make this claim is a former Mormon.[24]

Polygamy

Perhaps the most embarrassing part of Mormon theology is their doctrine of plural marriages and their widespread practice of it until the United States Government made it virtually impossible for them to continue.

"And again, as pertaining to the law of the priesthood—if any man espouse a virgin, and desire to espouse another, and the first give her consent, and if he espouse the second, and they are virgins, and have vowed to no other man, then he is justified; he cannot commit adultery for they are given unto him; for he cannot commit adultery with that that belongeth unto him and to no one else. And if he have ten virgins given until him by this law, he cannot commit adultery, for they belong to him, and they are given unto him; therefore he is justified."[25]

One of the problems with this infamous section is that it stands in stark contrast to the explicit teaching of *The Book of Mormon* itself in which polygamy was absolutely prohibited. "Behold, David and Solomon truly had many wives and concubines, which thing was abominable before me, saith the Lord . . . For there shall not any man among you have save it be one wife; and concubines he shall have none; For I, the Lord God, delight in the chastity of women."[26]

It should go without saying that the whole concept of the monogamous marriage customs of the western world are based directly on the teachings of the Bible.

The Manifesto

Modern Mormons will protest that they no longer believe in plural marriages and they may quote the famous Manifesto by Wilford Woodruff. "Inasmuch as laws have been enacted by Congress forbidding plural marriages, which laws have been pronounced constitutional by the court of last resort, I hereby declare my intention to submit to those laws, and to use my influence with the members of the Church over which I preside to have them do likewise."[27]

It is impossible to read Section 132 and the Manifesto without observing that the commands regarding plural marriages are presented as a direct revelation from God whereas the Manifesto is nothing more than an official declaration that was voted on and accepted by the church. In defending their own position against polygamy, the Reorganized Church points out that the Utah Mormons have never removed Section 132 from their *Doctrine and Covenants*. "They still hold to a *belief* in the divinity of the doctrine while renouncing its present *practice*."[28]

Anyone who knows the events which immediately preceded the Manifesto against polygamy, cannot help but see that it was done as a result of pressure from the government not on the basis of moral principles. In the year 1882, the Edmunds Act prohibited the practice of polygamy by law. In 1887, the Edmunds-Tucker Act stiffened the enforcing of the laws against polygamy and in 1896, Utah became a state. The Manifesto, therefore, appears to have been the price The Latter-day Saints had to pay for the inclusion of Utah in the States.

Although Mormons are forced to admit the facts of their own history, they attempt to gloss it over by saying that plural marriages were never very common even when they were permitted. "Never at any time were more than *three percent* of the families of the Church polygamous."[29] Despite this statement, the same author virtually contradicts himself when he protests the pressure that the American Government exerted against plural marriages. "The law was administered with extreme harshness. Thousands of Mormons were disfranchised. A thousand men were imprisoned because they had plural families."[30] It should be remembered that this was at a time when the Mormon Church had not attained anywhere near the membership that it has today but even then the laws against polygamy affected thousands of Mormons.

The Encyclopaedia Britannica claims that Joseph Smith himself was a polygamist.[31] *Fortune* magazine credits Brigham Young, the second prophet, with having had twenty-seven wives and fifty-six children.[32] Wilford Woodruff, the prophet who issued the Manifesto against polygamy, was himself a polygamist.[33] Joseph Fielding Smith, a nephew of the first prophet and President of the church in 1901, was tried in court for polygamy in 1907 and fined $300 after the birth of his forty-third child.[34]

Thus it can be seen that modern Mormon writers have had to admit the widespread practice of polygamy. Completely objective secular sources state the polygamy of the early leaders of the church as a simple historical fact and the adherents of the Reorganized Church are convinced that the Utah

Mormons still believe in plural marriages but do not practice them.

The Reorganized Church leaders indicate their belief that the Utah Mormons would revert to the practice of plural marriages if they could gain sufficient political strength. "... the matter still remains a live issue, the more so in the light of statements made privately by certain of their men that they hope some day to hold the balance of political power in enough states so they can secure a modification of the laws touching polygamy in a way to permit a renewal of its practice. Such statements tend to keep the issue alive and project it into the political as well as the religious arena."[3][5]

Mormonism and God

Mormons believe that God was once a man and that any man may eventually become a god. They put it in the form of a sort of axiom. "As man is, God once was; as God is, man may become."[3][6] Thus, Mormons must admit that they believe in the existence of many gods. Of course, this stands in stark contrast to the monotheistic religions of the world, such as Mohammedanism, Judaism and Christianity. If there is any one doctrine that is abundantly clear in the Bible, it is the truth that there is only one God. All other gods that are mentioned are figments of the imagination of idolatrous man.

"Ye are my witnesses, saith the Lord, and my servant whom I have chosen: that ye may know and believe me, and understand that I am he: before me there was no God formed, neither shall there be after me" (Isaiah 43:10).

Jesus reaffirms this Old Testament principle when He says: "The first of all the commandments is, Hear, O Israel; The Lord our God is one Lord" (Mark 12:29).

It is evident that the people to whom He was speaking accepted this as a declaration of monotheism because when they answered they said: "Well, Master, thou hast said the truth: for there is one God; and there is none other but he" (Mark 12:32).

The Apostle Paul also declared his belief in the monotheism of both Judaism and Christianity when he said: "We know that an idol is nothing in the world, and that there is none other God but one" (1 Corinthians 8:4).

When a Mormon missionary finally admits that the Church of the Latter-day Saints is indeed polytheistic in its view of God, he will usually counter by saying that the Bible accepts the existence of other gods. It is a fact that in many places throughout Old and New Testaments other gods are mentioned. However, the Apostle Paul clarified this issue in exactly the same Epistle to the Corinthians when he said: "For though there be that are called gods, whether in heaven or in earth, (as there be gods many, and lords many,) But to us there is but one God, the Father, of whom are all things, and we in him; and one Lord Jesus Christ, by whom are all things, and we by him" (1 Corinthians 8:5-6).

All the Apostle has done here is to state a fact of history—namely that men have created their own gods. In other words, they are gods by human creation not by actual existence.

God is Physical

Mormons teach that God has a physical body of flesh and bones that is just as real as man's. "The Father has a body of flesh and bones as tangible as man's."[37]

One of the arguments that they use to support their flesh and bone God is the fact that throughout all of the Scriptures He is described as having the ability to see, hear, walk, feel, and so on. They go on to say that the Bible states that God has hands, arms, feet, eyes and ears. In other words, because God is described as doing many of the things that men do and having the same physical characteristics as men, Mormons conclude that God must of necessity actually have a flesh and bone body like man's.

What they fail to say is that God is described in terms of other material things as well as the physical features of man. For instance, the Psalmist says about God: "He shall cover thee with his feathers, and under his wings shalt thou trust" (Psalm 91:4). But we have never heard the Mormons claim that God is some kind of bird with feathers and wings.

In the New Testament, Jesus is described as a Door, a Shepherd, a Vine, a Roadway and a Loaf of Bread but even the Mormons realize that these are figures of speech and are not intended to mean that Jesus is a material door, shepherd, vine, roadway or loaf of bread.

Apart from the inconsistency of Mormon logic, the Bible makes it apparent for all to understand that God is definitely not physical but He is pure Spirit: "God is a Spirit: and they that worship him must worship him in spirit and in truth" (John 4:24).

No translation that is true to the original languages can change the force of this statement and no interpretation that is true to the context can add to the Spirit of God a physical body. The Samaritan woman believed that God had to be worshipped in a given place as if He had a body and could only be in one place at a time. "Our fathers worshipped in this mountain; and ye say, that in Jerusalem is the place where men ought to worship" (John 4:20). The answer Jesus gave showed that God is not confined to a physical body but that He can be everywhere at one and the same time because He is pure Spirit.

The descriptions of God in the Bible are usually in one of two categories: sometimes they are theophanies where God takes on some physical form in order to contact an individual, or they may be anthropomorphisms where the Bible describes God in terms of a man so that we can understand something about Him.

One of the wildest claims of Mormonism is that the God of the Bible came into the world as Adam and then gradually ascended to the position of God. "When our father Adam came into the Garden of Eden, he came into it with a celestial body, and brought Eve, one of his wives, with him. He helped to make and organize the world . . . he is our father and our God, and the only God with whom we have to do."[38]

The Doctrine of The Trinity

When it comes to this cardinal doctrine of the Christian Faith, Joseph Smith seems to contradict himself. In *The Book of Mormon* he supports it but in his preaching he denies it.

"And now, behold, my beloved brethren, this is the way; and there is none other way nor name under heaven whereby man can be saved in the Kingdom of God. And now, behold, this is the doctrine of Christ, and the only and true doctrine of the Father, and of the Son, and of the Holy Ghost, which is one God, without end. Amen."[39]

In his sermon on the plurality of gods which he preached on June 16, 1844, Joseph Smith says, "I have always declared God to be a distinct personage, Jesus Christ a separate and distinct personage from God the Father, and that the Holy Ghost was a

distinct personage and a Spirit: and these three
constitute three distinct personages and three
Gods."[40]

To sum it up, Mormonism is a polytheistic religion.
It teaches that God changes—He was once a man and
man can become a god. The God of the Bible came
into the world as Adam and he still has a body of
flesh and bones just like a man. Its doctrine of the
Trinity is completely different from the teaching of
the Bible.

Jesus Christ and the Virgin Birth

Brigham Young taught that Jesus was not begotten
by the Holy Ghost but that Adam who had become
God had physical intercourse with the virgin Mary
and Jesus was the result. "He was *not* begotten by the
Holy Ghost . . . Jesus our elder brother was begotten
in the flesh by the same character that was in the
Garden of Eden and who is our father in heaven."[41]

Bear in mind that Brigham Young, along with
Joseph Smith and each of the other presidents of the
Mormon Church, are considered prophets and any
new revelation that they have is considered just as
authoritative as any of their other sacred writings.

Orson Hide was one of the twelve apostles under
the original prophet, Joseph Smith. He taught that
Jesus married Martha and both of the Marys and saw
His children before He was crucified.[42]

In Mormon theology, it is difficult to discern any
real difference between Jesus Christ and any other
man. Both are thought by Mormons to have had an
existence before birth, both have a period of testing
as human beings on this earth, and both can become
gods in the next life. If there is any difference
between Jesus Christ and other men, it is one of time
rather than nature.

The Mormons and Negroes

Mormon theology puts Negroes and Indians in a class by themselves. As opposed to all the other peoples of the world, Negroes cannot become priests and little, if any, missionary work is done among the Negro people in the African countries.

Joseph Smith established this pattern in *The Pearl of Great Price:* "For behold, the Lord shall curse the land with much heat, and the barrenness thereof shall go forth forever; and there was a blackness came upon all the children of Canaan, that they were despised among all people . . .

"And Enoch also beheld the residue of the people which were the sons of Adam; and they were a mixture of all the seed of Adam save it was the seed of Cain, for the seed of Cain were black, and had not place among them."[43]

The Latter-day Saints are among the most outstanding missionary organizations in the world. They boast that they have more than thirteen thousand workers but it would appear that little is done to reach the Negro world.

The fact that Negro men are not permitted to be priests becomes a serious point of discrimination when we remember that every male member twelve years of age and upwards is a priest, except in extremely rare circumstances. Any man who is not a priest is strictly a second-class citizen.

In a recent interview with Martin O'Malley, the President of the Canadian Mission of The Church of Jesus Christ of Latter-day Saints, Mr. Lamont Toronto, was quoted as saying, "Through revelation to Joseph Smith (founder of the church) it's been a policy since the beginning of our church that Negroes could not hold the priesthood 'til such time as the Lord gave our prophet a new revelation."[44]

In this world of extreme racial pressure and consciousness, the handwriting is already on the wall as far as this particular part of Mormon belief is concerned. In all probability, just as they gave in to the demands of the United States Government in regard to polygamy, they will eventually have to give in to the pressure that must be coming from all sources in connection with the Negro. We may live to see a new Manifesto in the very near future.

Conclusion—Salvation

The Mormon way of salvation is summed up in verse four of *The Articles of Faith.* "We believe that the first principles and ordinances of the Gospel are: first, Faith in the Lord Jesus Christ; second, Repentance; third, Baptism by immersion for the remission of sins; fourth, Laying on of hands for the gift of the Holy Ghost."[45] Rather than arguing the validity of this statement regarding the way of salvation, it will be more profitable for us to confine ourselves to the Bible—the One Book that Mormons as well as others consider to be the authoritative Word of God.

The best-known verse in the Bible is found in the Gospel of John. "For God so loved the world, that he gave his only begotten Son, that whosoever believeth in him should not perish, but have everlasting life" (John 3:16).

"He that believeth on him is not condemned: but he that believeth not is condemned already, because he hath not believed in the name of the only begotten Son of God" (John 3:18).

"He that believeth on the Son hath everlasting life: and he that believeth not the Son shall not see life; but the wrath of God abideth on him" (John 3:36).

When the Philippian jailer asked Paul and Silas how

he could be saved, their answer was simple. "Believe on the Lord Jesus Christ, and thou shalt be saved" (Acts 16:31).

The Book of Romans was written by the Apostle Paul to re-assert this truth that was first preached by Jesus Christ and His disciples—that salvation was by faith in Christ and it was a result of the grace of God. "Therefore being justified by faith, we have peace with God through our Lord Jesus Christ"(Romans 5:1).

As we approach the end of the Bible, salvation by faith in Christ is proclaimed once again. "These things have I written unto you that believe on the name of the Son of God; that ye may know that ye have eternal life, and that ye may believe on the name of the Son of God" (1 John 5:13).

The thief on the cross had no time to be baptized, he had never kept the law and there was no opportunity of piling up a record of good works, but when he turned to Christ, Jesus was quite firm in saying: "Today shalt thou be with me in paradise" (Luke 23:43).

FOOTNOTES

[1] Seymour Freedgood, "Mormonism: Rich, Vital, and Unique", *Fortune,* Vol. LXIX, No. 4, p. 136.

[2] *Time,* January 19, 1962, Vol. LXXIX, No. 3, p. 56.

[3] Walter R. Martin, *The Maze of Mormonism* (Grand Rapids: Zondervan Publishing House, 1962), p. 18.

[4] Joseph Smith, *The Pearl of Great Price* (Salt Lake City: Church of Jesus Christ of Latter-day Saints, 1949), "Writings of Joseph Smith", 2:18 & 19, p. 48.

[5] Gordon B. Hinckley, *What of the Mormons?* (Salt Lake City: Church of Jesus Christ of Latter-day Saints, 1949), p. 23.

[6] *Census of Canada,* "Population, Religious Den-

ominations" (Ottawa: Dominion Bureau of Stastics, 1961), Catalogue 92-546, Vol. 1—Part 2, p. 4-1.

[7] Einar Anderson, *I Was a Mormon* (Grand Rapids: Zondervan Publishing House, 1966), p. 29.

[8] Anthony A. Hoekema, *The Four Major Cults* (Grand Rapids: William B. Eerdmans Publishing Company, 1963), p. 13.

[9] Ibid., p. 85.

[10] *The Book of Mormon* (Salt Lake City: The Deseret Book Company, 1966), III Nephi 2: 27, p. 422 (quotations are from my copy of *The Book of Mormon* presented and inscribed to me by Lamont F. Toronto, President of The Mormon Church in Canada, Sep. 17, 1967).

[11] Ibid., III Nephi 11:33-34.

[12] Le Grand Richards, *A Marvelous Work and a Wonder* (Salt Lake City: Deseret Book Company, 1966), p. 73.

[13] Ibid., p. 75.

[14] Martin, *The Maze of Mormonism,* p. 46.

[15] Ibid., pp. 46-47.

[16] *The Book of Mormon,* I Nephi 16:18, p. 32.

[17] Ibid., 18:12, p. 39.

[18] Hoekema, *The Four Major Cults,* p. 18.

[19] Ibid., p. 19.

[20] Ibid., pp. 19, 84 and 85.

[21] *The Book of Mormon,* I Nephi 11:21, p. 19.

[22] Hoekema, *The Four Major Cults,* p. 23.

[23] *The Book of Mormon*, Alma 7:10, pp. 211—212.

[24] Anderson, *I Was a Mormon,* p. 25.

[25] *The Doctrine and Covenants* (Salt Lake City: The Church of Jesus Christ of Latter-day Saints, 1965), Section 132, verses 61—62, p. 245.

[26] *The Book of Mormon*, Jacob 2:24, 27—28, p. 111.

[27] *The Doctrine and Covenants,* p. 257.

[28] Elbert A. Smith, *Differences that Persist*

(Independence: Herald House, 1950), p. 16. (Elbert A. Smith in 1950 was the Presiding Patriarch of the Reorganized Church of Jesus Christ of Latter-day Saints.)

[29] Hinckley, *What of the Mormons?*, p. 24.

[30] Ibid, p. 209.

[31] *Encyclopaedia Britannica* (New York: Encyclopaedia Britannica Company, eleventh edition, 1911), Vol. 18, p. 844.

[32] *Fortune*, April 1964, Vol. LXIX, No. 4, p. 137.

[33] *Encyclopaedia Britannica*, Vol. 18, p. 846.

[34] Ibid., p. 847. (It is interesting to notice that in the 1967 edition these statements on the polygamy of the Mormon Church leaders are omitted. The article on "The Latter-day Saints" in Volume 13 is written by three residents of Utah—obviously Mormons themselves.)

[35] Smith, *Differences that Persist*, p. 16.

[36] Ibid., p. 9. (Quoted from *The Articles of Faith* by James E. Talmage (Salt Lake City: Deseret News Press, 1901, pp. 442 and 443.)

[37] *The Doctrines and Covenants*, Section 130, verse 22, p. 238.

[38] Smith, *Differences that Persist*, p. 10. (quoted from *Journal of Discourses* by Brigham Young, Vol. 1, p. 50).

[39] *The Book of Mormon*, II Nephi 31:32, p. 105.

[40] Hoekema, *The Four Major Cults*, p. 35.

[41] Martin, *The Maze of Mormonism*, p. 96 (quoted from *Journal of Discourses*, Vol. I, pp. 50 and 51).

[42] Ibid., p. 111.

[43] Smith, *The Pearl of Great Price*, Moses 7:8 and 22, pp. 20 and 21.

[44] *The Globe and Mail*, Toronto, June 24, 1967, p. 44

[45] Hoekema, *The Four Major Cults*, p. 60 (quoted from *The Articles of Faith* by James E. Talmage).

CHAPTER V

WHO ARE JEHOVAH'S WITNESSES AND WHAT DO THEY BELIEVE?

Jehovah's Witnesses have some extremely commendable characteristics and no assessment of their movement or their doctrines would be fair that did not take into consideration and recognize their value.

In a generation of widespread uncertainty, it is rather refreshing to find a group of people such as these who are deeply convicted about what they believe. It seems that it has become fashionable these days to be rather uncertain about everything. As a matter of fact, the dogmatic person is looked upon as if he were some undesirable element in society. Whatever else the Christian faith may be, there is no doubt that it is dogmatic. There is no more dogmatic book in the world than the Bible. The basic principles of the Word of God leave no room for personal opinion, private interpretation or double meaning.

Examples of this are to be found in the words of Jesus: "I am the way, the truth and the life: no man cometh unto the Father, but by me" (John 14:6). In the words of the Apostle Peter: "Neither is there salvation in any other: for there is none other name under heaven given among men, whereby we must be saved" (Acts 4:12). In the words of the Book of Hebrews: "Without shedding of blood is no remission" (Hebrews 9:22).

Right or wrong Jehovah's Witnesses at least have the courage of their convictions and they are not afraid to stand for something regardless of the opinion of other people. This indeed is a credit to the entire movement.

Jehovah's Witnesses have a familiarity with the Scriptures that is sadly lacking among many evangelical Christians. Our people are sometimes an easy prey for the Witnesses simply because they do not have an adequate grasp of the teaching of the Bible and even if they do, they seldom know where to find the passages with which they are familiar. For instance, it would be refreshing if our people knew as much about why they believe in the doctrine of the Trinity as Jehovah's Witnesses know about why they do not believe in it. This would apply to all of the basic doctrines of the Church that are denied by the Watchtower Society—the Deity of Christ, the Atonement, the personality of the Holy Spirit, etc.

Jehovah's Witnesses are impelled by a great sense of urgency that has been lost by the majority of the members of the Christian churches. Of course, the liberal churches have long since lost any sense of urgency because of their exclusive emphasis upon social reconstruction rather than the preaching of the Gospel of Christ. Sad to say, some of our evangelical people have been contaminated by the same deadly disease. On the other hand, Jehovah's Witnesses believe that the Battle of Armageddon is just around the corner and the day of opportunity is quickly passing away. Thus, they move out with a zeal that is often sadly lacking in our ranks.

Jehovah's Witnesses are not afraid to be different. They are willing to stand on street corners, knock on doors and witness for their cause whenever they have an opportunity. Most of us have a tendency to want to be accepted—in our business, in our schools, on our street and amongst our friends. However, the milestones of the Christian Church have been laid primarily by men and women who stood alone in the face of opposition, ridicule and sometimes death.

"That is the preachment believed implicitly by Jehovah's witnesses. It fires them to zeal. They live in an atmosphere of urgency that keeps growing. They drop every other hope, aspiration, and work in this world to devote their lives and resources and time and energies to preaching it."[1]

Perhaps as a direct result of some of these commendable characteristics, Jehovah's Witnesses may be the fastest growing religious group in the world. In the year 1901 there were 101 of them in the Dominion of Canada. Sixty years later there were 68,018.[2]

According to one of their official books, "During the decade 1942-52 the number of Jehovah's Witnesses doubled in North America, multiplied five times in Asia, more than six times in the Pacific Islands, about seven times in Europe and Africa, more than twelve times in the Atlantic Islands, and nearly fifteen times in South America."[3]

Pastor Russell

The story of Jehovah's Witnesses can be told under the names of their three leaders. The Founder, organizer and first prolific writer of the movement was Charles Taze Russell. He was a Congregationalist who lived about sixty-four years and established this group which is now less than one hundred years old. He was married but had no children and his wife sued for divorce in 1913 on the grounds of "his conceit, egotism, domination, and improper conduct in relation to other women."[4]

It should be remembered that the early history of any movement is not of necessity the criterion of its present value. There are many organizations that had a fine beginning and have deteriorated seriously and vice versa. Harvard University is a good example of a school that was founded on the principles of historic Christianity and is today almost completely sold out to Unitarianism. On the other hand, the science of astronomy has to look for its beginnings to the rather questionable practice of astrology.

Thus, the early history of any religious movement is by no means the final test of its worth. However, history cannot be ignored and certainly it should not be re-written. Unfortunately, many of the new groups that claim to be Christian have a tendency to gloss over some of the questionable people and events that were a part of their early years. This is the sin of the totalitarian nations. It should not be the sin of a religious group.

Judge Rutherford

When Pastor Russell died on October 31, 1916, he was succeeded by Judge Joseph Franklin Rutherford, a Baptist who lived seventy-three years and was largely responsible for the transition of Jehovah's Witnesses from a democracy to a theocracy. It was during the twenty-five years of his Presidency that the group became officially known as Jehovah's Witnesses. They based this on the words of the Old Testament: "Ye are my witnesses, saith the Lord, and my servant whom I have chosen" (Isaiah 43:10).

President Knorr

When Judge Rutherford died on January 8, 1942, Nathan Homer Knorr became the President—a position which he holds at the time of writing (1969) when he is approximately sixty-four years of age.

Amongst other things, it has been during the years of Knorr's presidency that the movement has spread far and wide throughout the entire world and at the same time has adopted a policy of publishing its literature without identifying the authors. Pastor Russell and Judge Rutherford were relatively well-known by the outside world but Nathan Knorr is known primarily by those in the ranks of the movement itself.

The Bible

Basic to a study of the doctrines of any organization is its position on the Word of God. As is the case with most of the newer groups that have departed from the historical doctrines of the Christian Church, Jehovah's Witnesses claim to believe in the absolute authority of the Bible. "To let God be found true means to let God have the say as to what is the truth that sets men free. It means to accept His Word, the Bible, as the truth. Hence, in this book, our appeal is to the Bible for truth. Our obligation is to back up what is said herein by quotations from the Bible for proof of truthfulness and reliability."[5]

This affirmation sounds thoroughly evangelical until one reads a few paragraphs of any Watchtower literature and discovers that instead of letting the Bible lead them to the truth, they take their doctrines and arbitrarily impose them upon the Bible. One of the ways in which they do this is by actually adjusting the translation. Jehovah's Witnesses have their own Bible. It is called the *New World Translation of the Holy Scriptures* and it claims to have been "Rendered from the Original Languages by the New World Bible Translation Committee—Revised A.D. 1961."[6] In accordance with their policy of publishing all of their material anonymously they have not listed the names of the people who produced their translation of the Scriptures. This is an important fact because it means we have no indication whatsoever of the credentials of the translators. We do not know whether they were outstanding Greek and Hebrew scholars or whether they were men with a limited language training who worked from other translations, commentaries and interlinear editions of the Bible.

In the case of the other major translations of the Bible, it is not difficult to learn who the translators were and in some cases their names are actually listed in every copy of their versions—*The American Standard Version* names the Secretaries of both the Old and New Testament companies; *The New English Bible* names the Chairmen and the Secretaries of the Translation Committee and the Chairman of the Joint Committee; *The Revised Standard Version* lists the names and qualifications of all the Committee Members since 1937.

The Deity of Christ

Jehovah's Witnesses deny the Deity of Jesus Christ and they try desperately in their *New World Translation* to adjust those passages that obviously equate Jesus and God. In the first verse of John's Gospel, their translation reads: "In (the) beginning the Word was, and the Word was with God, and the Word was a god" (John 1:1, *New World Translation*).[7]

Their explanation of this change is that when the word "God" appears first in this verse, it is preceded by a definite article but the second time it does not have a definite article. Therefore, the first should be translated "God" and the second "a god." This explanation becomes inconsistent when we note that the word "God" (theos) appears without the definite article at least four times in this same chapter and in each case the *New World Translation* is "God", not "a god" (verses 6, 12, 13 and 18). However, the Watchtower Society choose to violate the scholarly principles of Greek translation used by hundreds of qualified men. The major translations read as follows:

King James: "In the beginning was the Word, and the Word was with God, and the Word was God."

New English Bible: "When all things began, the Word already was, The Word dwelt with God, and what God was, the Word was."

American Standard Version: "In the beginning was the Word, and the Word was with God, and the Word was God."

Revised Standard Version: "In the beginning was the Word, and the Word was with God, and the Word was God."

New Testament in the Language of the People, Charles B. Williams: "In the beginning the Word existed; and the Word was face to face with God; yea, the Word was God Himself."

In connection with the Deity of Christ, it is quite obvious that Jehovah's Witnesses have not translated the Bible. They have imposed their peculiar doctrines on the Bible and called it a translation.

It would be difficult to read the Bible without realizing that the Holy Spirit is always presented as a person not an impersonal force. That is why all the scholarly translations of the ancient manuscripts refer to the Holy Spirit as *he, him* and *who*. Jehovah's Witnesses do not believe in the personality of the Holy Spirit and they inflict this belief on the Sacred Scriptures by using the pronouns *it, which* and *that* instead of the personal pronouns which are demanded by the context of the passages that deal with the activities of the Holy Spirit (see their translation of Romans 8:16 and Ephesians 4:30).

Absurd Applications

Another way in which they distort the teaching of the Bible is by making applications that are not intended or implied. One of these which has received a considerable amount of publicity in the press is their position on blood transfusions. All Bible students are aware of the fact that God forbade the Jewish people to eat blood. One of the basic passages is to be found in the Book of Leviticus: "And whatsoever man there be of the children of Israel, or of the strangers that sojourn among you, which hunteth and catcheth any beast or fowl that may be eaten; he shall even pour out the blood thereof, and cover it with dust. For it is the life of all flesh; the blood of it is for the life thereof: therefore I said unto the children of Israel, Ye shall eat the blood of no manner of flesh: for the life of all flesh is the blood thereof: whosoever eateth it shall be cut off" (Leviticus 17:13-14).

On the basis of passages such as this, Jehovah's Witnesses adamantly refuse to have blood transfusions either for themselves or their children. There is nothing wrong with any religious group that rejects some medical practice. However, the point is that the rejection of blood transfusions cannot be based upon these passages. In the first place, it is obvious that the Bible is talking about the blood of animals not humans. It is also obvious that it is talking about eating the blood—that is taking it into the body through the mouth. This is quite different from a transfusion in which human blood is injected directly into the veins.

Fantastic Types

The Word of God is further complicated by the use of some of the most fantastic types imaginable. In the story of the rich man and Lazarus, they see the rich man as the clergy of Christendom and Lazarus as Jehovah's Witnesses. Babylon is modern Christendom. The "beast" (Revelation 16) is the Roman Catholic Church. The God of Babylon (Jeremiah 51) is the Pope. The Image of the Beast (Revelation 13:14) is the Protestant Federation of Churches. The two-horned Beast (Revelation 13:11)is the Church of England, and the Mark of the Beast is the claim of apostolic authority held by the Roman Catholic and Anglican Churches, and the right of ordination practised by the Protestant Churches.[8]

Arbitrary Transitions

Jehovah's Witnesses' major method of confusing the teaching of the Bible can best be described by the words arbitrary transitions. By this I mean their habit of jumping about from passage to passage in the Bible in a manner that is not even remotely implied by the proof texts involved.

One of their basic prophetic beliefs is that Jesus Christ returned in the year 1914 and established His Kingdom on the earth. They arrive at this particular date in the most amazing manner. In chapter twenty-one of their standard book, *Let God be True*, they start with Matthew 24:3, jump to Mark 13:4, then again to Luke 21:24, back to Daniel 4, forward to Revelation 12:6 and 14, and back to Ezekiel 4:6. On the basis of these verses combined with some mathematics that would make Dr. Einstein's hair stand on end, they conclude, "Therefore, since God's typical kingdom with its capital at Jerusalem ceased to exist in the autumn of 607 B.C., then, by counting the appointed times from that date, the 2,520 years extend to the autumn of A.D. 1914."[9]

If some poor soul were to be left with nothing but a Bible, he would not have a hope of arriving at the year 1914 for the Second Coming of Christ. As a matter of fact, this is exactly what Pastor Russell believed: ". . . people cannot see the divine plan in studying the Bible by itself . . . if anyone lays the 'Scripture Studies' aside . . . and ignores them and goes to the Bible alone, though he has understood the Bible for ten years, our experience shows that within two years he goes into darkness. On the other hand, if he had merely read the 'Scripture Studies' with their references and had not read a page of the Bible as such, he would be in the light at the end of two years, because he would have the light of the Scriptures."[10]

Doctrines Denied

Jehovah's Witnesses deny almost every doctrine of historical Christianity:

"The trinity doctrine was not conceived by Jesus or the early Christians. Nowhere in the Scriptures is even any mention made of a trinity."[11] This of course involves their denial of the Deity of Jesus Christ and the Deity of the Holy Spirit.

"The body (of Jesus) was not permitted to corrupt. Hence Jehovah God disposed of that body in his own way, just as he disposed of the body of Moses, who was a type of Christ Jesus; but no one knows how."[12] (Parenthesis mine.) "His perfect human life, with all its rights and prospects, was laid down in death, but not for sin and in punishment. It was not taken back by Jesus at his resurrection, for he was raised a divine spirit creature."[13]

"It is a settled Scriptural truth, therefore, that human eyes will not see him at his second coming, neither will he come in a fleshly body."[14]

"A.D. 1914 marks the time when he came to the temple as King ... The truth of his coming then was first discerned by the Scriptures and by the fulfillments of prophecy after the event, namely, first in 1922."[15]

These excerpts from Watchtower publications indicate clearly that Jehovah's Witnesses deny the doctrines of the Trinity, the Deity of Christ, the Deity of the Holy Spirit, the bodily resurrection and the Second Coming. Anyone who reads the Bible will see very quickly that it contradicts the teachings of the Watchtower Society. It takes a considerable amount of crafty manipulation from outside sources to eliminate any of these basic doctrines from the Bible.

The Soul

Perhaps the most enticing of the Watchtower denials of Scripture is their complete rejection of the Bible's teaching about hell. This depends upon their view that man does not have a soul or spirit that goes on living after his body has died. Jehovah's Witnesses believe that man is a soul or a spirit—in other words that he has a body in which there is a life principle.

"The claim of religionists that man has an immortal soul and therefore differs from the beast is not Scriptural ... There is not one Bible text that states the human soul is immortal ... even the man Christ Jesus was mortal. He did not have an immortal soul: Jesus, the human soul, died."[16]

Jehovah's Witnesses are quite right in stating that there is no place in the Bible that says the human soul is immortal. However, it is also true that no text in the Bible says that Jesus Christ will return in the year

1914. Nor is there a text that says man will live forever on this earth. And nowhere in the Bible does it say that this earth will last forever. However, Jehovah's Witnesses believe and teach each of these last three opinions.

The fact that there is a part of man which goes on living after his body is dead and buried is expressed in many different chapters. Jesus said: "Fear not them which kill the body, but are not able to kill the soul: but rather fear him which is able to destroy both soul and body in hell" (Matthew 10:28).

When this verse is quoted, Jehovah's Witnesses are quick to point out that it clearly supports their position—that death means the destruction or annihilation of the whole man, body and soul. As a matter of fact, this is precisely what is stated in their book, *Let God Be True*. "Since God destroys soul and body in Gehenna, this is conclusive proof that Gehenna, or the valley of the son of Hinnom, is a picture or symbol of complete annihilation, and not of eternal torment."[1 7]

It is not difficult to show that the word *appolumi* in the New Testament never means annihilate. Sometimes it means to be lost. It is used in connection with the lost sheep, the lost coin, and the lost son (Luke 15). In each of these stories, the Greek verb is describing something that is separated from its rightful owner—not something that has been annihilated.

Sometimes it means to become useless. It is used in connection with the old wineskins and the waste of money when ointment was poured on Jesus' head (Matthew 9:17 and 26:8). Once again there is no thought of annihilation but rather something that is not in its proper place.

Sometimes *appolumi* means to kill. Herod was

seeking to destroy the Child Jesus (Matthew 2:13). Certainly it is obvious that killing is not annihilation.

Thus, when Jesus speaks about the possibility of the destruction of the soul and body in hell, He cannot possibly be talking about annihilation unless the Greek word at this point takes on a special meaning that it does not have anywhere else in the New Testament, and of course this does not happen in any language unless there is some very probable explanation for it.

In the Book of Revelation, there is a passage that quite clearly teaches the existence of a soul after the body has been killed. "And when he had opened the fifth seal, I saw under the altar the souls of them that were slain for the word of God, and for the testimony which they held: And they cried with a loud voice, saying, How long, O Lord, holy and true, dost thou not judge and avenge our blood on them that dwell on the earth? And white robes were given unto every one of them; and it was said unto them, that they should rest yet for a little season, until their fellowservants also and their brethren, that should be killed as they were, should be fulfilled" (Revelation 6:9-11).

It is quite clear that these verses are talking about souls that are alive after their bodies had been killed in martyrdom. It is obvious that this is not a description of something that has happened after the resurrection because the blood of these people has not yet been avenged nor have their brethren on the earth completed their course. These souls are very much alive and they are still waiting for the final consummation.

The Greek word that is used in both of these passages is *psuchee*. Jehovah's Witnesses argue that since this word usually refers only to mortal life as it is found in both men and animals, it cannot possibly refer to a part of man that goes on living after his body has died. In other words, they think the Greek word *psuchee* has only one meaning. Contrary to this idea, one of the most modern Greek-English lexicons by F. Wilbur Gingrich, published by the University of Chicago Press in 1965, gives the following definitions for the word: *"the soul* as seat and center of the inner life of man in its many and varied aspects, desires, feelings, emotions . . . *the soul* as seat and center of life that transcends the earthly."[18]

Pneuma

The other Greek word that must come into this discussion is *pneuma* which is generally translated spirit. It is used by Jesus on the cross: "Father, into thy hands I commend my spirit" (Luke 23:46).

Jehovah's Witnesses counter this by saying that spirit here means power of life but the fact of the matter is that pneuma never means power of life.[19]

The martyr, Stephen, uses a similar expression: "And they stoned Stephen, calling upon God, and saying, Lord Jesus, receive my spirit" (Acts 7:59). When Jesus spoke to the thief on the cross, He made it clear that although his body was about to be killed, the thief would go immediately to be with Him in paradise. "And Jesus said unto him, Verily I say unto thee, Today shalt thou be with me in paradise" (Luke 23:43).

The other major versions of the Bible, including *The New English, The Revised Standard* and even Jehovah's Witnesses' *Emphatic Diaglott,* confirm this translation. However, the *New World Translation* stands alone in changing this passage so that it reads: "And he said to him: 'Truly I tell you today, You will be with me in Paradise'."[20]

When the thief asked his question, he expressed it in such a way that he expected Jesus to remember him *when* He came into His Kingdom—or at the end time. Jesus' words of comfort to this man indicated that He did not have to wait until the resurrection but that very day he would be with Him in paradise. The rendering of the *New World Translation*—in opposition to other versions—is another attempt to make the Word of God fit Watchtower theology.

The Apostle Paul

The Apostle Paul obviously expected to be with Jesus Christ when He died: "For I am in a strait betwixt two, having a desire to depart, and to be with Christ; which is far better: Nevertheless to abide in the flesh is more needful for you" (Philippians 1:23-24).

Paul believed that he could be in his body or with the Lord. For him departure from the body meant to be present with the Lord and the Greek construction makes this quite clear. The verbs "to depart" and "to be" are linked in a Greek sequence of verbs and articles that indicate two aspects of the same thing. There is no time lapse between them.[21] He drives this home with great conviction by declaring that death is "gain" and it is "far better." By what stretch of the imagination could Paul have thought that annihilation was better than life?

The Apostle Paul sets forth exactly the same truth in his letter to the Corinthians. "Therefore we are always confident, knowing that, whilst we are at home in the body, we are absent from the Lord . . . We are confident, I say, and willing rather to be absent from the body, and to be present with the Lord" (II Corinthians 5:6 and 8).

Once again the Greek verbs are set in a form that

makes it clear that the transfer is instantaneous. There is no thought of annihilation or a long sleep or a period of oblivion between leaving the body and joining the Lord.

The Doctrine of Hell

Once Jehovah's Witnesses have rid themselves of the idea of a soul that goes on living after death, it is not too difficult for them to equate death with hell and thus eliminate the scriptural teaching of eternal punishment.

" 'What a horrible and disgusting subject! I do not want to discuss it. I have no desire to hear anything about that infernal place. We have plenty of hell here. Please do not start on such a subject!' In disgust so exclaimed a woman with whom one of Jehovah's Witnesses was conversing. Do you blame this woman for expressing herself in such a way? We do not. It would be natural for her to speak so, and also for all those who have been taught by Christendom to believe the God-dishonoring doctrine of a fiery hell for tormenting conscious human souls eternally."[2 2]

Playing upon the average person's fear of hell, Jehovah's Witnesses go on to comfort them and incidentally win converts by saying, "It is so plain that the Bible hell is mankind's common grave that even an honest little child can understand it, but not the religious theologians . . . The doctrine of a burning hell where the wicked are tortured eternally after death cannot be true, mainly for four reasons: (1) It is wholly unscriptural; (2) it is unreasonable; (3) it is contrary to God's love, and (4) it is repugnant to justice."[2 3]

Their basic argument against hell is to point out the places in the Old Testament where the word *sheol* means nothing more than the grave and that where it is translated in our English versions by the word hell, it still means the grave. As far as Jehovah's Witnesses are concerned, hell is the grave and the grave is hell. Both are described by the word *sheol*. "Since *hell* means mankind's common grave or the pit of burial, it could not at the same time mean a place of fiery torture or a place of two compartments, one of bliss and one of fiery torment."[24]

Once again Jehovah's Witnesses have slipped into the error of concluding that a word can only mean one thing or that it always means the same thing. Of course, this is not true in any language. Most of our English words may mean many different things. In Webster's New Collegiate Dictionary, the word *runt* is defined in at least five different ways—an old crow, an old, withered woman, any animal that is unusually small, the dead stump of a tree or the stem of a plant.[25] All of these things can be expressed by one word because they have at least one thing in common. The context makes it clear which of the meanings is intended.

The Hebrew word *sheol* can mean grave, pit, or hell. Because these have some common factors, they can be expressed by the same word but the places involved do not have to be the same. It is the context of the passage that determines which is intended. Certainly the word *sheol* in the Old Testament does not always mean grave. As a matter of fact, it has a great variety of meanings. "If I ascend up into heaven, thou art there: if I make my bed in hell, behold, thou art there" (Psalm 139:8). Surely, the Psalmist does not think of God being in the grave. In this passage hell (*sheol*) is obviously contrasted with heaven. It has nothing to do with the grave.

"Out of the belly of hell (*sheol*) cried I, and thou heardest my voice" (Jonah 2:2). Here is another example where *sheol* in the Old Testament does not mean grave. Jonah was not in the grave and he was certainly not buried.

The Rich Man and Lazarus

Jehovah's Witnesses believe that the story of the rich man and Lazarus was a parable and they have a rather fantastic interpretation of it that reads something like this: "The rich man, every reader can see, pictured the highly favored, self-important religious leaders, who find their counterpart today in the religious clergy of Christendom. The beggar, whose name 'Lazarus' means 'God is helper', pictured that Jewish remnant who hungered and thirsted for truth and righteousness and who depended upon the religious leaders for spiritual nourishment . . .

"By means of God's angels the beggar class were transferred to Abraham's household to feast with him at his table, leaning upon his bosom. This meant becoming free from dependence on Jewish religious leaders . . . The religious rich man class died to their former advantageous condition and came into torments instead of comforts . . . The rich man class were buried in Hades, Sheol, or hell or the grave (all equivalent terms) in that they were rejected from God's service and were just as inactive in it as persons in the grave are inactive, buried in earthly things . . . In their dead and buried condition the religious rich man class were subject to fiery torment. How? By exposure to the teaching of God's Word by Jesus and his disciples . . .

"In what way, then, did they want the Lazarus class to dip the tip of their finger in water and cool the tongue of those tormented in the blazing fire? Since water is used as a symbol of Scriptural truth, they wanted the Lazarus class to leave the bosom of

God's favor and compromise the truth and present the message of God's Word in such a way as not to torment them any further . . . the rich man class prayed God to send the remnant to his 'five brothers', that is, his allies and religious associates, that he 'may give them a thorough witness'. By this the rich man class indirectly acknowledged that the remnant are Jehovah's Witnesses."[2 6]

This, of course, is an arbitrary interpretation that is not to be found implied in the actual story that Jesus told. There is no possibility that a person could read this passage and come to these same conclusions without a great deal of prodding and suggestion and twisting of the actual text by outside sources.

How much easier it is simply to accept the story as Jesus told it—what happens to people after they die.

Conclusion

Despite their futile attempts to eliminate the concept of eternal punishment in hell from the Scriptures, they find themselves powerless to do so. Like any other major teaching, it may be interpreted out of one section but it remains immovable in others. Three passages quoted directly from the *New World Translation* make it abundantly apparent to any honest reader that the Bible teaches the fact of eternal punishment, quite apart from any thought of annihilation.

1) In connection with the wheat and tares, Jesus says: "Therefore, just as the weeds are collected and burned with fire, so it will be in the conclusion of the system of things. The Son of man will send forth his angels, and they will collect out from his kingdom all things that cause stumbling and persons who are doing lawlessness, and they will pitch them into the fiery furnace. There is where (their) weeping and the gnashing of (their) teeth will be."

In the same chapter, Jesus uses the illustration about the good and bad fish in the same manner: "That is how it will be in the conclusion of the system of things: the angels will go out and separate the wicked from among the righteous and will cast them into the fiery furnace. There is where (their) weeping and the gnashing of (their) teeth will be."[2 7]

2) When someone asked Jesus about the number of people who would be saved, He answered: "Exert yourselves vigorously to get in through the narrow door, because many, I tell you, will seek to get in but will not be able, when once the householder has got up and locked the door, and you start to stand outside and to knock at the door, saying, 'Sir, open to us.' But in answer he will say to you, 'I do not know where you are from.' Then you will start saying, 'We ate and drank in front of you, and you taught in our broad ways.' But he will speak and say to you, 'I do not know where you are from. Get away from me, all you workers of unrighteousness!' There is where (your) weeping and the gnashing of (your) teeth will be, when you see Abraham and Isaac and Jacob and all the prophets in the kingdom of God, but yourselves thrown outside."[2 8]

3) In the Book of Revelation the same truth is emphasized in crystal clear language: "And another angel, a third, followed them, saying in a loud voice: 'If anyone worships the wild beast and its image, and receives a mark on his forehead or upon his hand, he will also drink of the wine of the anger of God that is poured out undiluted into the cup of his wrath, and he shall be tormented with fire and sulphur in the sight of the holy angels and in the sight of the Lamb. And the smoke of their torment ascends forever and ever, and day and night they have no rest, those who worship the wild beast and its image, and whoever

receives the mark of its name. Here is where it means endurance for holy ones, those who observe the commandments of God and the faith of Jesus.' And I heard a voice out of heaven say: 'Write: Happy are the dead who die in union with (the) Lord from this time onward. Yes, says, the spirit, let them rest from their labors, for the things they did go right with them'."[29]

Only by doing theological handsprings can any honest reader avoid the Biblical pronouncement of eternal punishment upon the wicked. Death is obviously something quite different from this.

FOOTNOTES

[1] Marley Cole, *Jehovah's Witnesses* (New York: Vantage Press, 1955), p. 23.

[2] *Canadian Census*, p. 41–1.

[3] Cole, *Jehovah's Witnesses*, p. 25.

[4] Hoekema, *The Four Major Cults*, p. 227.

[5] *Let God Be True* (Brooklyn: Watchtower Bible and Tract Society, 1952), p. 9.

[6] *New World Translation of the Holy Scriptures* (Brooklyn: Watchtower Bible and Tract Society, 1961), p. 3.

[7] Ibid., John 1:1, p. 1151.

[8] George D. McKinney, *The Theology of The Jehovah's Witnesses* (Grand Rapids: Zondervan Publishing House, 1962), pp. 36 and 37.

[9] *Let God Be True*, pp. 250, 251 and 252.

[10] Walter R. Martin and Norman H. Klann, *Jehovah of the Watchtower* (New York: Biblical Truth Publishing Society, 1953), p. 22, quoted from *The Watch Tower*, Sep. 15, 1910, p. 298.

[11] *Let God Be True*, p. 111.

[12] *The Truth Shall Make You Free* (Brooklyn:

Watchtower Bible and Tract Society, 1943), pp. 263—264.

[13] *Let God Be True,* p. 113.

[14] *The Truth Shall Make You Free,* p. 295.

[15] Ibid., pp. 301 and 302.

[16] *Let God Be True,* pp. 68, 69 and 71.

[17] Ibid., p. 99.

[18] F. Wilbur Gingrich, *Shorter Lexicon of The Greek New Testament* (Chicago: University of Chicago Press, 1965), p. 239.

[19] Hoekema, *The Four Major Cults,* p. 349.

[20] *New World Translation,* Luke 23:43, p. 1149.

[21] Hoekema, *The Four Major Cults,* p. 354. Authority for this statement from A.T. Robertson, *Grammar of the Greek Testament in the Light of Historical Research* (Nashville: Broadman Press, 1934), p. 787.

[22] *Let God Be True,* p. 88.

[23] Ibid., pp. 92 and 99.

[24] Ibid., pp. 89 and 90.

[25] *Webster's New Collegiate Dictionary,* p. 742.

[26] *What Has Religion Done for Mankind?* (Brooklyn: Watchtower Bible and Tract Society, 1951), pp. 249, 250, 251, 252, 253 and 254.

[27] *New World Translation,* Matthew 13:40—42 and 49—50, p. 1069.

[28] Ibid., Luke 13:24—28, p. 1135.

CHAPTER VI

SPIRITUALISM—CAN THE LIVING COMMUNICATE WITH THE DEAD?

" Spiritualism is the Science, Philosophy and Religion of continuous life, based upon the demonstrated fact of communication between this world and the Spirit world by means of mediumship, and a Spiritualist is one who endeavours to mould his/her character and conduct in accordance with the highest teachings derived from such communications.

"A Medium is one whose organism is sensative to vibrations from the Spirit world and through whose instrumentality, intelligence in that world are able to convey messages and produce the phenomena of Spiritualism."[1]

Spiritualism is probably as old as the history of man, certainly as old as the Bible. It would be difficult to find any civilization that did not have some elements of Spiritualism in it. However, the modern Spiritualist movement can be dated from the year 1848 when Margaret and Kate Fox claimed to have made contact with a spirit whom they called "old splitfoot." This together with some other rather strange phenomena was supposed to have taken place in Hydesville, New York, which is a sort of mecca for Spiritualists.

A great deal can be said for the validity of the claims of Spiritualists. A number of cases have been documented by rather responsible persons who seem to believe unequivocally that there is considerable evidence that Spiritualist Mediums can actually do the things they claim. On the other hand, there is an equally impressive list of rewards that have been offered to Spiritualist Mediums if they can prove the validity of their claims and these rewards have never been collected. Our purpose is not to assess the validity of Spiritualists' claims but simply to point out the teaching of the Word of God about communication between the physical world and the spirit world. In the many passages that touch on this subject, three basic truths become apparent.

Communication Possible

The Bible accepts the fact that communication between the spirit world and the physical world is possible. According to their own recorded testimonies, the Apostles Paul, Peter and John were permitted to have some contact with the spirit world while they were still alive in this world.

The Apostle Paul tells his story in these words: "I knew a man in Christ above fourteen years ago, (whether in the body, I cannot tell; or whether out of the body, I cannot tell: God knoweth;) such an one caught up to the third heaven. And I knew such a man, (whether in the body, or out of the body, I cannot tell: God knoweth;) How that he was caught up into paradise, and heard unspeakable words, which it is not lawful for a man to utter" (II Corinthians 12:2–4).

The Apostle Peter's story is told in the Book of Acts. "On the morrow, as they went on their journey, and drew nigh unto the city, Peter went up upon the housetop to pray about the sixth hour: And he became very hungry, and would have eaten: but while they made ready, he fell into a trance, And saw heaven opened, and a certain vessel descending unto him, as it had been a great sheet knit at the four corners, and let down to the earth: Wherein were all manner of fourfooted beasts of the earth, and wild beasts, and creeping things, and fowls of the air. And there came a voice to him, Rise, Peter; kill, and eat. But Peter said, Not so, Lord; for I have never eaten anything that is common or unclean. And the voice spake unto him again the second time, What God hath cleansed, that call not thou common. This was done thrice: and the vessel was received up again into heaven" (Acts 10: 9–16).

John's experience is recorded in the Book of Revelation. "After this I looked, and, behold, a door was opened in heaven: and the first voice which I heard was as it were of a trumpet talking with me; which said, Come up hither, and I will shew thee things which must be hereafter. And immediately I was in the spirit: and, behold, a throne was set in heaven, and one sat on the throne" (Revelation 4:1–2).

In each of these stories the men involved were still on this earth and they went on living in their physical bodies for some time afterwards but it is quite obvious that they were permitted to see and to hear something from the world of the spirit. Paul, Peter and John had some sort of communication with the next world.

These are examples of the barrier being broken in the direction of the physical to the spiritual.

There are also a number of instances recorded in the Bible where the barrier between the two worlds is broken in the other direction—from the spiritual to the physical. All of the appearances of angels that are recorded both in the Old and New Testaments prove that the barrier between the spiritual world and the material world is not impenetrable. Angels are spirit beings and they have made themselves known to men who are physical beings.

The Book of Hebrews certainly gives us every reason to believe that in some manner God's people who have died and gone to heaven are cognizant of what is going on here in this world. After cataloguing the great men and women of the Old Testament who died in the faith in the eleventh chapter, the twelfth begins in this way: "Wherefore seeing we also are compassed about with so great a cloud of witnesses, let us lay aside every weight, and the sin which doth so easily beset us, and let us run with patience the race that is set before us" (Hebrews 12:1). Of course this passage could refer only to the witness that was left by these people in the Scriptures. On the other hand, it is difficult to read these two chapters consecutively without visualizing a sports arena in which those of us who are still in our bodies are on the race course and God's people who have died are in the grandstand.

When the rich man asked Abraham to send Lazarus back to warn his five brothers who were still living, Abraham did not ridicule his request as impossible. He simply said it would not do any good: "If they hear not Moses and the prophets, neither will they be persuaded, though one rose from the dead" (Luke 16:31).

Of course the classic example in the New Testament of communication from the world of the spirit to the world of the physical is in the story of the Transfiguration: "And after six days Jesus taketh Peter, James, and John, his brother, and bringeth them up into an high mountain apart, And was transfigured before them: and his face did shine as the sun, and his raiment was white as the light. And, behold, there appeared unto them Moses and Elias talking with them" (Matthew 17:1-3).

At this time Jesus, as well as Peter, James and

John, were still living in their physical bodies on this earth and Moses and Elijah who had been dead for hundreds of years appeared and talked with Jesus. Obviously this is an example of men who had been in the spirit world for a long time breaking through the barrier so that they could be seen and heard by men who were still in the physical world.

Saul at Endor

In the Old Testament, the classic example of this phenomenon is the story of King Saul and the Spiritualist Medium at Endor. In this account King Saul consulted a woman who had a "familiar spirit." In the course of events Samuel actually appeared and predicted Saul's final doom. "Now Samuel was dead, and all Israel had lamented him, and buried him in Ramah, even in his own city. And Saul had put away those that had familiar spirits, and the wizards, out of the land.

"And the Philistines gathered themselves together, and came and pitched in Shunem: and Saul gathered all Israel together, and they pitched in Gilboa.

"And when Saul saw the host of the Philistines, he was afraid, and his heart greatly trembled.

"And when Saul enquired of the Lord, the Lord answered him not, neither by dreams, nor by Urim, nor by prophets.

"Then said Saul unto his servants, Seek me a woman that hath a familiar spirit, that I may go to her, and enquire of her. And his servants said to him, Behold there is a woman that hath a familiar spirit at Endor.

"And Saul disguised himself, and put on other raiment, and he went, and two men with him, and they came to the woman by night: and he said, I pray thee, divine unto me by the familiar spirit, and bring me him up, whom I shall name unto thee.

"And the woman said unto him, Behold, thou knowest what Saul hath done, how he hath cut off those that have familiar spirits, and the wizards, out of the land: wherefore then layest thou a snare for my life, to cause me to die?

"And Saul sware to her by the Lord, saying, As the Lord liveth, there shall no punishment happen to thee for this thing.

"Then said the woman, Whom shall I bring up unto thee? And he said, Bring me up Samuel.

"And when the woman saw Samuel, she cried with a loud voice: and the woman spake to Saul, saying, Why hast thou deceived me? for thou art Saul.

"And the king said unto her, Be not afraid: for what sawest thou? and the woman said unto Saul, I saw gods ascending out of the earth.

"And he said unto her, What form is he of? And she said, An old man cometh up; and he is covered with a mantle. And Saul perceived that it was Samuel, and he stooped with his face to the ground, and bowed himself.

"And Samuel said to Saul, Why hast thou disquieted me, to bring me up? And Saul answered, I am sore distressed; for the Philistines make war against me, and God is departed from me, and answereth me no more, neither by prophets, nor by dreams: therefore I have called thee, that thou mayest make known unto me what I shall do.

"Then said Samuel, Wherefore then dost thou ask of me, seeing the Lord is departed from thee, and is become thine enemy?

"And the Lord hath done to him, as he spake by me: for the Lord hath rent the kingdom out of thine hand, and given it to thy neighbour, even to David:

"Because thou obeyedst not the voice of the Lord, nor executedst his fierce wrath upon Amalek, therefore hath the Lord done this thing unto thee this day.

"Moreover the Lord will also deliver Israel with thee into the hand of the Philistines: and to morrow shalt thou and thy sons be with me: the Lord also shall deliver the host of Israel into the hand of the Philistines.

"Then Saul fell straightaway all along on the earth, and was sore afraid, because of the words of Samuel: and there was no strength in him; for he had eaten no bread all the day, nor all the night" (I Samuel 28:4–20).

Many attempts have been made to explain this phenomenon. Some suggest that a demon took the form and voice of Samuel. Others think that Saul was in such a weakened condition his confused mind made him imagine he saw Samuel. He had not eaten for twenty-four hours. Others believe it was a pure case of deception on the part of the woman. However, the Bible makes no attempt to explain the incident. It simply describes it as factual. The woman saw Samuel. King Saul knew it was Samuel and recognized his voice. If the story is accepted as it stands in the Word of God, then it is an example of a man who lived in the spirit world breaking through the barrier and communicating with a King who was still in the physical world.

God Initiates Communication

Although the Bible accepts the possibility of some kind of contact between the two worlds, it gives us no reason to believe that man knows how to communicate with the dead. In every case where there is any interaction between the spiritual world and the physical world, God in some form initiates it. Man has nothing whatever to do with it.

In the case of the appearances of the angels, God sends them. When Paul was "caught up to the third heaven", he was completely passive in the whole process. He refers to it as one of the "revelations of the Lord."

When Peter saw heaven opened, he had fallen into a trance and once again it is quite obvious that Peter had absolutely nothing to do with initiating either the trance or the vision.

When John was permitted to look into heaven, he describes what he saw as "the revelation of Jesus Christ."

In the story of the Transfiguration, we have an account of God in the form of Jesus Christ using his divine power to initiate the appearance of Moses and Elijah. Peter, James and John were nothing more than observers.

Finally, in the Old Testament story of King Saul, it would be impossible to read it without realizing that the sudden appearance of Samuel came as a great shock to the Spiritualist Medium. Apparently this sort of thing was not something to which she was accustomed because the Bible says: "when the woman saw Samuel, she cried with a loud voice." The simplest explanation is that God initiated the re-appearance of Samuel in order to predict the final doom of Saul.

There is no evidence in the Bible that any living man has ever had the power to contact the spirit of any departed person. But the Bible makes it clear that God does have this power and we have discussed a number of examples which have been recorded. None of these required the power of a Spiritualist Medium.

Where a Spiritualist Medium is involved, his success

may be a result of three things. There may be some validity to mental telepathy—the power of one mind to know what is going on in another mind. Although this may be very real and quite possible, it should be remembered that mental telepathy has nothing whatever to do with communication between the living and the dead. It involves communication between two persons who are still in the physical world.

The second reason for success may lie in the fact that the Medium is a good magician or a plausible fortune teller. This probably explains ninety-five percent of the "phenomena" that is attributed to Spiritualist Mediums. There is very little that any of them do that cannot be duplicated by an expert magician.

On Saturday, October 21, 1967, one of my friends whom we will call operative "47" had a private seance with a Spiritualist Medium in the City of Toronto, Canada. The Medium was in her mid-seventies and spoke with an English accent. The entire seance was tape recorded and the next day I listened to it from beginning to end. Obviously the Medium was nothing more than a relatively good gypsy fortune teller. She simply asked a series of well thought out questions. If she got a negative answer from "47", she simply dropped that question and moved on to another. If she got an affirmative answer, she would ask a second question along the same line. Once again, if the answer to the second question was negative, she dropped the subject and then asked some other question. Her initial questions were all extremely general, so much so that they would apply to almost anybody: "Have you had some disappointment in your life? Was there someone near to you that was in the First or Second World Wars?"

It is interesting to note that this Spiritualist Medium did not make statements but only asked questions. An unsuspecting person who was emotionally disturbed could quite easily have fallen into the trap and given her a great deal of information in every answer. Such a person would have gone away from the seance thinking that the Medium had told him something miraculous when in fact she had revealed nothing but the answers he had already given her himself.[2]

This is undoubtedly the basic explanation of the majority of Spiritualist Mediums as far as their apparent success is concerned. However, there may be a small percentage who actually succeed in producing psychic phenomena which are a direct result of demon power. This is one of the reasons that we should avoid any consultation with Spiritualist Mediums. Ninety-five percent of them are probably fakes but a small percentage are the tools of the Devil and should be avoided by Christians.

The Bible Condemns Mediums

Man is commanded to make no attempts to communicate with the spirit world. This practice is severely condemned throughout the entire Bible and the whole impact of Scriptural teaching along this line is that people who are in contact with God have no need to communicate with departed spirits.

The Bible makes it clear that King Saul did not consult the Spiritualist Medium at Endor until after he had completely lost his contact with God. "And when Saul enquired of the Lord, the Lord answered him not, neither by dreams, nor by Urim, nor by prophets. Then said Saul unto his servants, Seek me a woman that hath a familiar spirit, that I may go to her, and enquire of her" (I Samuel 28:6—7).

"So Saul died for his transgression which he committed against the Lord, even against the word of the Lord, which he kept not, and also for asking counsel of one that had a familiar spirit, to enquire of it; And enquired not of the Lord: therefore he slew him, and turned the kingdom unto David the son of Jesse" (I Chronicles 10:13—14).

Other passages in the Bible make this same truth apparent: "Regard not them that have familiar spirits, neither seek after wizards, to be defiled by them: I am the Lord your God" (Leviticus 19:31). In this verse, the choice is between familiar spirits and the Lord God.

"And the soul that turneth after such as have familiar spirits, and after wizards, to go awhoring after them, I will even set my face against that soul, and will cut him off from among his people. Sanctify yourselves therefore, and be ye holy: for I am the Lord your God. And ye shall keep my statutes, and do them: I am the Lord which sanctify you" (Leviticus 20:6—8). Here the choice is between familiar spirits and holiness.

"And ye shall be holy unto me: for I the Lord am holy, and have severed you from other people, that ye should be mine. A man also or woman that hath a familiar spirit, or that is a wizard, shall surely be put to death: they shall stone them with stones: their blood shall be upon them" (Leviticus 20:26—27). Once again the contrast is between familiar spirits and holiness.

"When thou art come into the land which the Lord thy God giveth thee, thou shalt not learn to do after the abominations of those nations. There shall not be found among you any one that maketh his son or his daughter to pass through the fire, or that useth divination, or an observer of times, or an enchanter, or a witch, or a charmer, or a consulter with familiar spirits, or a wizard, or a necromancer. For all that do these things are an abomination unto the Lord: and because of these abominations the Lord thy God doth drive them out from before thee. Thou shalt be perfect with the Lord thy God. For these nations, which thou shalt possess, hearkened unto observers of times, and unto diviners: but as for thee, the Lord thy God hath not suffered thee so to do. The Lord thy God will raise up unto thee a Prophet from the midst of thee, of thy brethren, like unto me; unto him ye shall hearken" (Deuteronomy 18:9–15). Here the choice is between a familiar spirit and a Prophet of God. It is interesting to notice that in this passage Spiritualist Mediums are put in the same category as people who sacrifice their children in the fire.

In the New Testament, witchcraft is listed as one of the works of the flesh: "Now the works of the flesh are manifest, which are these; Adultery, fornication, uncleanness, lasciviousness, Idolatry, witchcraft, hatred, variance, emulations, wrath, strife, seditions, heresies" (Galatians 5:19–20).

When the Apostle Paul visited Philippi, he was followed by a girl who had a familiar spirit and he drove the spirit out in the Name of Jesus Christ (Acts 16:16–19). Familiar spirits and the Son of God cannot live within the same person.

Conclusion

We may draw three conclusions from the teaching of the Bible: 1) The Bible takes it for granted that communication between the spirit world and the physical world is possible. 2) The instances of such communication that are recorded in the Bible are all initiated by God. There is no Scriptural evidence that any man is able to communicate with departed spirits. Whenever some modern Mediums seem to be successful, it must be attributed to trickery or demon power. 3) The Bible forbids man to make any attempts to communicate with departed spirits and severely condemns Spiritualist Mediums.

FOOTNOTES

[1] J. Granted, *"The President's Message"* , The United Spiritualist Church of Ontario Syllabus, p. 11.
[2] A transcript of this tape is kept in my files.

CHAPTER VII

UNITARIANISM–AND THE ULTIMATE QUESTIONS OF LIFE

T here are many different kinds of cakes. They may be dark or light, large or small, round or square, chocolate or vanilla, and so on. However, there are certain basic ingredients that are essential to any cake. Or else we cannot call it a cake. It would be ridiculous to conclude that any one of these basic ingredients is a cake. In most cakes milk is an essential component. However, by no stretch of the imagination could we say that a glass of milk is a cake. It simply does not have the minimum requirements.

This is equally true in the realm of religion. There are some similarities among all religious groups. However, there are certain elements that are basic in each particular religion which give it a reason for existence. Mohammedanism can be identified by a certain combination of beliefs and practices that are peculiar to it. So can Judaism, Buddhism, Hinduism and Christianity. If a man calls himself by the name of any one of these religions, he must adhere at least to its minimum requirements.

The fact that a man is monotheistic does not give him the right to say that he is a Mohammedan. It takes a great deal more than the belief in one god to make a Mohammedan. The fact that a man believes in the principle of reincarnation is not sufficient grounds to call him a Hindu. It takes more than a belief in reincarnation to make a Hindu. The fact that a man may adhere to some of the ethics of Jesus does not give him the right to call himself a Christian. As is true in the case of Mohammedanism and Hinduism, it takes more than one element of Christianity to make a Christian.

In this area, the Unitarians of the world have done the Christian Church a great service. They are perhaps the only group which originated in the Christian Church but who dropped the name "Christian" when they realized that they no longer had the basic ingredients that are essential to Christianity.

Rev. Phillip Hewett, Minister of the Unitarian Church in Vancouver, British Columbia, says, "In most religious bodies there is an orthodoxy of belief which sets the norm, no matter how far individual members may stray from it in practice."[1]

Rev. Stephen H. Fritchman, Minister of the First Unitarian Church of Los Angeles, puts it this way: "There are quite specific meanings today for the word 'Christian'. The overwhelming majority of members of Christian churches around the world . . . believe that a Christian must have a firm faith in God, he must believe in the immortality of the soul, if not the resurrection of the body, and he must believe in Christ as saviour of the individual in the world to come."[2]

Because of this the majority of Unitarians no longer claim to be Christians. Certainly they have some of the characteristics of Christians and they may even believe some of the things that Christians believe, but they themselves do not feel that they have the minimum requirements that would be necessary if they were to consider themselves Christian. According to a survey of its members that was made by the Unitarian-Universalist Association, only twenty-nine per cent of its Canadian adherents claimed to be Christian while seventy-one per cent said they were not. The God of the Bible was accepted by three per cent and thirty per cent believed in no god at all. In all probability among the sixty-seven per cent who apparently claimed some sort of belief in God, their concept of God was an impersonal force or principle. The same survey revealed that ninety per cent did not believe in any kind of personal immortality after death.[3]

Unitarian History

Although Unitarianism concerns itself with many things today, it started in the early Church with a denial of the Deity of Jesus Christ. This, of course, is as old as the Bible and the Apostle John had to deal with it before the end of the first Christian century. "Hereby know ye the Spirit of God: Every spirit that confesseth that Jesus Christ is come in the flesh is of God: And every spirit that confesseth not that Jesus Christ is come in the flesh is not of God: and this is the spirit of antichrist, whereof ye have heard that it should come; and even now already is it in the world" (I John 4:2—3).

Nearly three hundred years later, the Church was confronted with it once again at the Council of Nicaea (A.D.325). It was known then as Arianism.

Although Unitarianism can be found in some form as far back as apostolic days, it was not represented by any theologians or writers until the Reformation. The first writer of any consequence was Martin Cellarius (1499—1564). He had been a friend of Martin Luther. In Italy Fausto Sozini (1539—1604) was the heretic. He is better known to most people as Socinus and his heresy is called Socinianism.

Unitarianism then spread to Poland and Hungary and by way of Holland to England. It was not until the eighteenth century that it appeared in the United States.

American Unitarianism was probably indigenous to the United States. It was a reaction against the extreme Calvinism and severe Puritanism of the New England States. As a matter of fact, the first Unitarians were called Arminians—not because their theology was Arminian but because they were in rebellion against Calvinism.

Encouraged by the modernism that was taking root in Germany during the nineteenth century, American Unitarianism flourished. In 1825 the American Unitarian Association was formed, in 1865 the National Conference was established and in 1960 the Unitarians merged with the Universalists. The official organ of the Unitarians was called *The Unitarian Register* and the Universalists published a magazine called *The Universalist Leader*. The merger of 1960 resulted in a combined magazine, *The Register-Leader*. [4]

Today there are approximately 157,000 Unitarians in the United States worshipping in 1,012 churches. In Canada there are approximately 20,000. [5]

What Do They Believe?

In the case of Jehovah's Witnesses or Christian Scientists or Mormons, it is relatively easy to outline their beliefs. However, this is not true of the Unitarians because they refuse to accept any sort of creed and their union is established by their diversity. In the area of religion, the common denominator seems to be a system of denials. They take a negative attitude towards almost every doctrine that has been held historically by the Christian Church. In the field of politics, it would seem that they tend to be opposed to the existing government and in the realm of social action, it would appear that they generally object to the status quo.

At this point one has a tendency to wonder if this kind of person might not be opposed to any doctrine, politics or way of life that was followed by the majority. In Canada 88.1% of the Unitarians voted either Liberal or New Democratic in the election of 1965.[6] However, if there should be a landslide of the entire country toward the New Democratic Party, we might discover that the Unitarians would be carrying the Conservative flag in the following election. It would seem that they revel in being opposed to the majority and are rather proud of the fact that they belong to a minority.

On the positive side, Unitarians are zealous worshippers at the shrines of science, reason, evolution and, above all, the human being. Sixty per cent of them are college graduates and twenty-five per cent hold graduate degrees. Someone has said, "You don't have to be a Ph.D. to be a Unitarian, but it helps."[7]

Social Action

Before the Unitarian General Assembly of 1967, a poll was taken of individual churches and fellowships regarding items that should be discussed. The consensus of opinion was as follows: Vietnam, the United Nations, the right to dissent, Draft Reform and conscientious objection, Congressional Reform, the Freedom Budget and the American Indian.[8]

At this point we might wonder why Unitarians still think of themselves as a religion, meet in buildings that are called churches and employ leaders that are ordained as ministers. As a matter of fact, apparently some of their own people are beginning to ask this question in many different ways. Peter Fleck, a New York investment banker who belongs to the First Unitarian Society of Plainfield, New Jersey, says:

"The task of the church is to serve as a link between the sacred and the secular, and its only justification as a church lies in bringing the things of the spirit into this world, thereby letting faith bring forth works, lest in the end man perish having neither."[9]

Although this writer is expressing the idea that a church must have a faith and a spiritual function, it would seem that his fear is a result of the fact that his own church has virtually lost its right to be called a church or a religion.

Certainly a church must have a sense of social responsibility but a sense of social responsibility by itself does not constitute a church or a religion. The tragedy not only of the Unitarian Church but also the modernistic church is that they have let the by-product become the product. Religion has to do with the relation of a man with his God. Social action will be the result of this relationship. The first is the product. The second is the by-product. If a man has faith, works will be the result. However, when he loses his faith, he loses his motivating force and in a very short time his works will come to naught.

Religion Without Angels

In a special issue of *The Register-Leader* describing the training programme for children in the Unitarian Church, it says: "Parents must be ready with imagination and honesty as well as sympathy for the child's emerging sensitivity to the natural world, a world full of religiously significant events wherein there is *no place for angels or devils.*"[10]

This is typical of the Unitarians' obsessive fear of the unknown—that is, anything they cannot explain scientifically or in accordance with man's sense of logic. This, of course, is precisely where Unitarianism breaks down as a religion. The whole being of man cries out for answers to the ultimate questions of life and he expects to find them in his religion. This is what the "search for truth" is all about. It is a quest for the truth about life itself. Where did I come from? Why am I here? Where am I going? And, who cares about me?

Several years ago I visited a life-long friend who was dying. When I arrived I found her alone in a private room, unconscious, breathing her last under an oxygen tent. I was not able to talk to her. She could not talk to me. As far as I know, she was not even aware of the fact that I was there. I watched her for a few minutes as she struggled for air and as I did so, my mind flashed back across the forty years that she had been such a dear friend and I remembered how much of herself she had given to me from the time I was fifteen months old until that moment.

Finally, I had to leave and as I turned to go, I thought, "My God, I can't leave her here like this to die alone." But she *was* alone. There was no nurse, no doctor, no relative and when I left, there would be no friend—nothing but a hospital bed, an oxygen tent, four walls and a few hours in which to die. It was at that moment that I remembered the promise of God,

"The angel of the Lord encampeth round about them that fear him, and delivereth them" (Psalm 34:7).

For most of a relatively long life, she had served God and in the very best sense of the word had feared the Lord and as I walked down that hospital corridor, I knew that whether she lived a few minutes, a few hours or a few days, she would not be alone when she died. The angel of the Lord would be there. When a Unitarian dies, he dies alone. There are no angels in his world.

What Do Unitarians Deny?

As we have already indicated, Unitarianism stresses the negatives not the positives. It is a system of religious denials rather than affirmations.

The springboard of Unitarian disbelief is their complete lack of confidence in the authority of the Bible. Rev. Kenneth Torquil MacLean of the Theodore Parker Unitarian Church in West Roxbory, Massachusetts, says: . "The Bible is accepted or rejected according to whether or not it has the right answers . . . to us the Bible is certainly a revelation of man's search for God in a particular tradition, but it is not *the* revelation . . . Understanding its historic role frees us to deal with the Bible as with any great collection of books—to read some of it and to ignore some of it; to look for its questions rather than its answers . . . Read the narratives and legends and myths as some of the attempts of a religiously gifted people to express the deepest questions and most profound experiences in life."[1] [1]

Once a man has rejected an authoritative view of inspiration, the writing is already on the wall, "Next Stop: Unitarianism." And as more and more Unitarians admit, from this position the next step is atheism.

The Deity of Jesus Christ

Although Unitarians deny almost every historic doctrine of the Christian Church, their name is derived from the fact that they do not believe in the Deity of Jesus Christ and, therefore, do not accept the Biblical doctrine of the Trinity. "Everything depends, in the Christian view, on knowing about and responding to Jesus Christ. And Christians know about him primarily through their churches or through the Bible . . . That is *the unique* revelation, as communicated by the one true book or the one true church . . . However, for many of us the central fact of religion and life is not Jesus Christ; our perceptions and reason and feelings do not lead us through that particular hourglass."[12]

Dr. Marshall E. Dimock, first moderator of the Unitarian Universalist Association, spells out his denial of the Deity of Jesus Christ in this way: "The great prophets are sons of God and no one of them is the only son of God because everyone is equally God's own."[13]

It is fortunate that the majority of Unitarians are honest enough at this juncture to admit that they can no longer be called Christians. The tragedy of the modern church is the fact that thousands of people who do not belong to the Unitarian Church believe exactly the same things. They refuse to accept the authority of the Scriptures and they demote Jesus Christ to the position of a great prophet. This is sad when it involves an ordinary man but it is gross dishonesty when it involves a man who poses as a Christian minister.

The great threat to the Christian faith is not the Unitarian on the outside of the Church. He is an honest man who is quite willing to stop using the name Christian that no longer applies to him. What is destroying the power of the modern church is the Unitarian on the inside who is garbed in the gown and stands in the pulpit of a Trinitarian. This man is a religious fifth columnist.

The Ultimate Questions

Some time ago I sat on a panel with a group of religious leaders to discuss hospital visitation with some student nurses. I was flanked by a Jewish Rabbi, a Roman Catholic Priest, a Liberal Minister and a Unitarian Minister.

After each of us had made a short presentation that attempted to describe our approach in the sick room, the girls were permitted to ask questions. It seemed that one of their greatest concerns could be expressed in the question, "What is your message to a dying man?"

In the Unitarian structure of thought, there really isn't any answer to this question because this is one of those ultimate problems that demands something science, reason and evolution cannot give. Unitarianism is built around the living. It has nothing to say to the dying. It would be interesting and pathetic to hear the response of a dying man to the philosophy of the Unitarian.

Perhaps he could bring comfort and confidence to his parishioner by reminding him that each generation of human beings in the process of their own evolution has made a better world for succeeding generations. This is a recurrent thought among Unitarians. They believe in the gradual development of the human being to his present state of enlightenment and that in the processes of nature, generations that are yet unborn will live in a much better world than ours. If there is no hope for the dying man personally, at least he might be buoyed up by the principle of evolution that says he has not lived in vain.

There are many problems with this approach to a man during his dying hours. It is highly questionable whether there is any real comfort at this time to be derived from the thought that things will be better in a few thousand years. In the second place, it is quite unrealistic to conclude that things in this world will be any better in succeeding generations. The history of our civilization to date gives just as much evidence for the decline of human civilization as it does for its progress.

When Martin Luther was stressing the necessity of justification by faith, there were Unitarians beginning to establish their "other gospel", but after nearly four hundred years Germany saw the rise of Naziism. One cannot help but wonder what the Unitarians of the Reformation period would have thought about the progress of man if they could have lived to see Hitler.

When John Wesley was preaching the Gospel in England and the whole of the British Isles was revolutionized socially as a result of it, there were Unitarians preaching this "other gospel." They too believed in the ultimate progress of man but one wonders what they would have thought about it had they lived long enough to walk the streets of Soho in 1970 and see the immorality, the nakedness and the addiction that has gripped the heart of London.

When Evangelist Billy Sunday was conducting his great crusades throughout the United States in the "roaring twenties", there were Unitarians preaching their "other gospel." Of course they recognized the tragic problems of their own generation but they believed that man in the long view was improving and that succeeding generations would be better. Once again, we wonder what these good people would say if they could have lived to read a 1967 issue of *U.S. News & World Report* which said in its lead article, "Conflict and violence are spreading across this country. There are more and more signs that what was to become the era of a 'Great Society' is turning instead into an era of strife."[14]

Or what would the Unitarians of Billy Sunday's day have said about the progress of the human race if they could have lived to read two successive issues of *Life* magazine that were headlined "Brazen Empire of Organized Crime—The Alarming Growth of a Multibillion-Dollar Cartel Founded on Corruption,

Terror and Murder . . . How the Mob Muscles Into Your Daily Life."[15]

Even when a man is dying he knows that the chances of the next generations being better than his are very slim indeed—that is, if he knows his history.

But perhaps the Unitarian minister would take another typical Unitarian approach and suggest to the dying man that he march to Washington carrying a sign protesting the war in Vietnam. If this did not work, he could suggest that he take a few thousand pamphlets on birth control and distribute them in India. In final desperation he might assure him that although he was about to die, he could do so knowing that in the future Jewish boys and girls would not have to listen to the New Testament in the public schools of Toronto.

This is not in any sense meant to disparage some of the good social action of a group of very fine people. It may be that many of these things should be done and are well worthwhile doing but the point is that when it is time to die, it is too late to take any kind of social action. There are many avenues open to the living but there is only one thing that the dying man can do—die. And there is only one question that is really important, How does a man get ready to die? At this point, Unitarianism has nothing to say.

The Word of God has some answers to the ultimate questions of life that make sense to the dying man. It tells him that his sins can be forgiven: "Through this man is preached unto you the forgiveness of sins" (Acts 13:38). This immediately solves one of man's greatest problems—guilt. Man walks through this life plagued by the guilt of his own shortcomings and when he arrives on his deathbed, the guilt is still there. If he has never learned it before, he needs to know now that through faith in Jesus Christ, he can die free of guilt.

The Bible tells the dying man that he can become a child of God: "But as many as received him, to them gave he power to become the sons of God" (John 1:12). He has lived the majority of his life among people who have not understood him. In his hours of deepest need, he has been absolutely alone, but now through faith in Jesus Christ, he can face death knowing that he will never be alone again. He is a child of God.

The Scriptures tell the dying man that he can have peace in his heart: "Therefore being justified by faith, we have peace with God through our Lord Jesus Christ" (Romans 5:1). He has lived his life in rebellion—against society, against ideas, against prejudices, against social injustice, against the Bible and against God. He has never known the meaning of peace but as he faces his final enemy, he can lay down his arms because through faith in Jesus Christ, he has made his peace with God.

Finally, the message of the Christian faith assures the dying man that when he closes his eyes on the scenes of this earth, he can open them in the presence of God: "Let not your heart be troubled: ye believe in God, believe also in me. In my Father's house are many mansions: if it were not so, I would have told you. I go to prepare a place for you. And if I go and prepare a place for you, I will come again, and receive you unto myself; that where I am, there ye may be also" (John 14:1—3).

These are the ultimate questions and the only ones that really concern us when we are dying—guilt, loneliness, judgment and eternity. Guilt is removed by forgiveness. Loneliness is dispelled by sonship. Judgment is satisfied by justification. Eternity is assured by Heaven. All of these are possible through a simple act of faith in Jesus Christ. The dying man cannot carry a placard or distribute pamphlets or read a book or listen to a lecture, but he can trust Jesus Christ as his Saviour.

FOOTNOTES

[1] Phillip Hewett, "Unitarians in Search of Goals", *Ferment '67,* Sep. 1967, p. 20, Vol. I, No. 1.

[2] Stephen H. Fritchman, "Are Unitarians Christians?", *The Register-Leader,* May 1967, p. 8, Vol. 149, No. 5.

[3] Hewett, "Unitarians in Search of Goals", p. 19.

[4] *The Encyclopaedia Britannica* (New York: The Encyclopaedia Britannica Company, 1911), Vol. 27, pp. 594-597.

[5] Allen Spraggett, "What Do Unitarians Believe?". *The Toronto Daily Star,* April 15, 1967, p. 15.

[6] Ibid.

[7] Hewett, "Unitarians in Search of Goals", p. 19.

[8] *The Register-Leader,* May 1967, p. 19.

[9] G. Peter Fleck, "Faith Without Works, Works Without Faith, Neither Will Do", *The Register-Leader,* Midsummer 1967, p. 4, Vol. 149, No. 7

[10] G.J. Melville-Whyte, "To Search", *The Register-Leader,* November 1963, p. 16, Vol. 145, No. 9.

[11] Kenneth Torquil MacLean, "How Should We Use the Bible?". *The Register-Leader*, Oct. 1963, pp. 8 and 9, Vol. 145, No. 8.

[12] Ibid.

[13] Marshall E. Dimock, "A Good Religion", Ibid., p. 11.

[14] *U.S. News and World Report,* Sep. 25, 1967, p. 41, Vol. LXIII, No. 13.

[15] *Life Magazine,* Sep. 1 and 8, 1967.

CHAPTER VIII

IS CHRISTIAN SCIENCE TRUE TO THE BIBLE?

I f I were witnessing on behalf of Christian Science, there are two areas that I would emphasize—their effective use of the printed page and their interest in healing.

In addition to a great many books, pamphlets and tracts which are coming off their presses by the thousands, the Christian Science Church publishes *The Christian Science Monitor* daily, *The Christian Science Sentinel* weekly, *The Christian Science Journal* and *The Herald of Christian Science* monthly, and *The Christian Science Quarterly.* Most of these are produced to promote the teachings of Christian Science primarily to their own constituents. However, the *Monitor* is recognized by the entire publishing world as one of the best and most reliable daily newspapers in existence.

In the area of healing of any kind, most of the church tends to be skeptical or at best fearful. On the one hand we are afraid of the extremes to which some of the itinerant faith healers have gone. On the other hand, many of us do not understand the psychological methods of Christian Science and, as a result, we have a tendency to dismiss healing as a possibility. However, the Bible includes it. A major part of the ministry of Jesus involved healing. The apostles travelled throughout the ancient world preaching the Gospel and healing people. In the extremely practical Epistle of James, healing is held forth as a genuine possibility and people are urged to call for the elders of the church and have them pray for the healing of their bodies: "And the prayer of faith shall save the sick, and the Lord shall raise him up" (James 5:15).

It should be noted at this point that the New Testament does not suggest miraculous healing as an exclusive method. Certainly, it does not rule out either doctors or medicine. Luke is referred to in the Bible as "the beloved physician" (Colossians 4:14). When the Apostle Paul was writing to Timothy, he did not advocate either prayer by the elders or mind over matter for Timothy's stomach trouble. He suggested a little wine which of course was recognized in those days not only as a beverage but for its medicinal qualities.

More will be said later about Christian Science and sickness but it is a fact that this emphasis has attracted a great many people to the Church of Christ, Scientist. The effective use of the printed page and the healing of the body are two of the most attractive aspects of Christian Science.

Unlike Mormonism, Christian Science is not promoted by missionaries in any real sense of the term. However, their churches have spread throughout most of the English-speaking countries of the world. There are approximately three thousand branches altogether and some eight thousand practitioners. Nearly two-thirds of these are in the United States and the others are to be found primarily in England, West Germany, Canada, Australia and New Zealand.[1]

According to the census of 1961, the Dominion Bureau of Statistics listed 19,466 members of the Church of Christ Scientist in Canada. This constitutes a slight drop from the 1951 figure of 20,795. In the City of Toronto there are 1,244 and it is interesting to notice that the majority of these are women—807 females and 437 males.[2] It is difficult to get an accurate count of Christian Science adherents because they do not list their memberships as do most other organizations. Thus these figures represent only those who claim to be Christian Scientists when a census is taken.

Mary Baker Eddy

The Founder of Christian Science was a rather remarkable woman best known to the world as Mary Baker Eddy. As a girl she was rather weak physically but she lived for eighty-nine years and founded a church that has lasted for nearly a hundred years and which simply cannot be ignored.

Perhaps the most effective way to tell the story of a woman's life is to relate it to her age and in the case of the Founder of Christian Science it would read something like this:

When she was seventeen she joined the Congregational Church at Tilton, New Hampshire and five years later, at the age of twenty-two, was married to George Glover. Her relationship with him was happy but short. He died six months after the wedding leaving his young wife with an unborn son.

When she was thirty-two, she was married for the second time to a dentist named Daniel Patterson. People who are interested in smearing the character of others should notice that there was nothing hasty or promiscuous about this marriage. A full ten years elapsed between the first and the second.

Perhaps far more important than her husbands was her meeting with Phineas P. Quimby. He had become relatively well-known in the area of Portland, Maine for his remarkable cures without the use of medicine. In the first instance Mrs. Eddy went to him about her own physical condition but, as we will note later, his work became an inseparable part of her system.

Quimby may have been the most important man she ever met but as far as the Founder was concerned, the most memorable incident in her life occurred when she was forty-five years of age. On February 1, 1866 she fell on the ice and within three days claimed a miraculous healing that was to be the basis of her church.

When she was fifty-two, she divorced Daniel Patterson. It should be noted here that he had deserted her and she did not divorce him until after they had been married for a total of thirteen years and until she had been separated from him as a result of the desertion for seven years.

The Christian Science textbook, *Science and Health with Key to the Scriptures*, was completed in the year 1875 when she was fifty-four years old and two years later she married Asa Gilbert Eddy, a sewing machine salesman. He was the first of her students to call himself a Christian Science practitioner. This marriage took place four years after her divorce from Daniel Patterson.

At the age of fifty-eight she incorporated the Church of Christ, Scientist and it was given a charter. Three years later, after they had been married for five years, Mr. Eddy died of a heart attack.

Many other exciting things took place in the life of this unusual woman but during her later years the two most important would be the publication of *The Christian Science Monitor* when she was eighty-seven years of age and her death on December 3, 1910 when she was eighty-nine.

Idealistic Philosophy

The basis of the entire Christian Science system is a denial of the existence of matter. In her writings, Mrs. Eddy expressed this in many different ways:

"The verity of Mind shows conclusively how it is that matter seems to be, but is not."[3]

"The mortal body is only an erroneous mortal belief of mind in matter. What you call matter was originally error in solution, elementary mortal mind."[4]

In her *Miscellaneous Writings*—a sort of secondary textbook for Christian Scientists—she suggests a series of questions and then gives the Christian Science answer. In connection with matter she asks the question, "How can I believe that there is no such thing as matter, when I weigh over two hundred pounds and carry about this weight daily?" Then she gives the answer, "By learning that matter is but manifest mortal mind."[5]

Diseases Do Not Exist

Once a person has accepted the idealistic philosophy that matter does not exist except in the form of mental error, it is very easy to progress to the idea that diseases do not exist either. Infection and germs are connected with our physical substance or the material that forms the body. If this material has no real existence, then oi ourse the infections and germs have none either.

For instance, a practitioner is urged to deal with consumption by pointing out that "it is not inherited; that inflammation, tubercles, hemorrhage, and decomposition are beliefs, images of mortal thought superimposed upon the body; that they are not the truth of man; that they should be treated as error and put out of thought. Then these ills will disappear."[6]

This method becomes rather humorous in the case of people who are overweight. Mrs. Eddy says, "that gluttony is a sensual illusion, and that this phantasm of mortal mind disappears as we better apprehend our

spiritual existence and ascend the ladder of life."[7]
For those who would like to curb their eating habits,
we might suggest some slogans: "It is mind, not
Metrecal, that will help you reduce. Throw away the
diet pills and think. Don't go hungry, use your head."

For those who might think the Christian Science
method of healing is effective only for those ailments
that are psychological, Mrs. Eddy claims, "One
disease is no more real than another. All disease is the
result of education, and disease can carry its ill-effects
no farther than mortal mind maps out the
way . . . Truth handles the most malignant contagion
with perfect assurance."[8]

She is quite consistent in her belief that her mental
methods apply to any sort of disease: "Destruction of
the auditory nerve and paralysis of the optic nerve are
not necessary to ensure deafness and blindness; for if
mortal mind says, 'I am deaf and blind,' it will be so
without an injured nerve."[9] This entire system is a
little difficult to comprehend, particularly if one has
some sort of an ailment that can be seen and felt,
such as a boil that is very physical and extremely
painful. But even in these circumstances the "leader"
sticks to her guns. "You say a boil is painful; but that
is impossible, for matter without mind is not painful.
The boil simply manifests, through inflammation and
swelling, a belief in pain, and this belief is called a
boil."[10]

The Founder's Claim to Revelation

Our purpose in quoting Mrs. Eddy's teaching about
disease is not to refute it. Most of us are quite aware
of the fact that there is a great deal of value in mental
therapy, particularly with certain kinds of illness. But
this remarkable woman claimed in no uncertain
words that her system was a direct revelation from
God and was original to her.

"In the year 1866, I discovered the Christ Science or divine laws of Life, Truth and Love, and named my discovery Christian Science. God had been graciously preparing me during many years for the reception of this final revelation of the absolute divine Principle of scientific mental healing."[1][1]

"No human pen nor tongue taught me the Science contained in this book, *Science and Health,* and neither tongue nor pen can overthrow it."[1][2]

"I have set forth Christian Science and its application to the treatment of disease just as I have discovered them. I have demonstrated through Mind the effects of Truth on the health, longevity, and morals of men; and I have found nothing in ancient or in modern systems on which to found my own, except the teachings and demonstrations of our great Master and the lives of prophets and apostles."[1][3]

It is not difficult to show that the Christian Science philosophy and system were not original with Mrs. Eddy. Many people for many years have expounded the same ideas but for the sake of brevity we must limit ourselves to five names.

George Berkeley

We have already identified Christian Science philosophy as idealistic and of course there have been a number of outstanding men who have written along this line. George Berkeley was an Irish philosopher who lived between 1685 and 1753—sixty-eight years before Mary Baker was born. Berkeley's idealism was summed up in the Latin motto, "Esse est percipi"—to be is to be perceived. In one of his treatises he elaborates on this by saying that "all those bodies which compose the mighty frame of the world, have not any subsistence without a mind—that their *being* is *to be perceived or known*; that, consequently, so long as they are not actually perceived by me, or do not exist in my mind or that of any other created spirit, they must either have no existence at all, or else subsist in the mind of some Eternal Spirit."[14]

In other words, the idealistic philosopher suggests that there may not be any objective world whatsoever and that it is there simply because our minds have the idea that it is there. Crudely illustrated we might say that when we face a person our sense of sight sees a form, our hearing senses sound and our hand gives us the idea of feeling. These combined with other sensations give us the idea that a material person is there. Now if we turn around and walk away, we can no longer see him, hear him or feel him. Therefore, suggests the idealist, he was not there in the first place and was never more than a subjective idea.

If you will go back and read our quotations from the pen of Mrs. Eddy, you will see that this is precisely the philosophy that she taught in regard to matter. It is nothing more than an illusion or idea of mortal mind. Why then, does she profess that this is original with her when every student of philosophy knows that it is not?

Plato

Pre-dating Mary Baker Eddy by more than 2,200 years was the Greek philosopher, Plato, who very definitely connected the mind with the healing of the body: ". . . For the body, as I conceive, is not the instrument with which they (physicians) cure the body; in that case we could not allow them ever to be or to have been sickly; but they cure the body with the mind, and the mind which has become and is sick can cure nothing."[15]

Franz Auton Mesmer

One of the pioneers in the field of hypnotism was an Austrian physician by the name of Franz Auton Mesmer. He was born in 1734 and died six years before the birth of Mary Baker. His theory of animal magnetism was referred to as Mesmerism and is now called hypnotism which more accurately describes the sleep-like condition of a person who is controlled by the mind of another.

Franz Mesmer shows that one individual can have a powerful influence over another. The Founder of Christian Science picked this up and added to it the word "malicious". This was her explanation of any physical defects that she had herself. Apparently she had false teeth, wore glasses and occasionally used morphine for her pain. In each case, she claimed that these were the result of "malicious animal magnetism"—the powerful effect of the mind of one of her enemies that caused her to think falsely that she had these physical disabilities.[16]

When her third husband died of a heart attack, she contested the autopsy and her physician confirmed her conviction that he had died of "arsenic poisoning mentally administered." The doctor involved was C.J. Eastman and when it was discovered that he had no medical credentials, he was sentenced to ten years in prison.[17]

Phineas Parkhurst Quimby

It is impossible to read even the official biographies of Mary Baker Eddy without realizing that Phineas Parkhurst Quimby constituted her basic source of material. She studied his methods of mental therapy very carefully, organized his ideas and put them into

the book that was to become "the Bible" of her
church.

One of the biographies published by The Christian
Science Publishing Society in 1930 gives considerable
recognition to Quimby. "His diagnosis in itself
increased her faith. He told her that she was 'held in
bondage by the opinion of her family and physicians,'
and 'her animal spirit was reflecting its grief upon her
body and calling it spinal disease' . . . Out of the
thirty-four hundred cases which Quimby treated in
those last two years at Portland only one at once felt
any obligation to pass on the healing gospel . . .
During those autumn weeks of 1862 she haunted
Quimby's office. She asked him questions. She read
all the notes accessible to those in whom Quimby
showed some interest. She studied his method."[18]

In the library of Union Theological Seminary in
New York City, there is a copy of a book written by
Horatio W. Dresser in which he quotes the Quimby
manuscripts. Those who have studied this volume say,
"We may say at once that, as far as the thought is
concerned, *Science and Health* is practically all
Quimby."[19]

Others who have studied the Quimby manuscripts
are not quite so kind in their objection and they
accuse Mrs. Eddy of plagiarism.

Georg Wilhelm Friedrich Hegel

The god of Christian Science is derived primarily
from the German philosopher, Georg Hegel. One of
the authorities on the philosophy of Hegel was Dr.
Francis Lieber. He wrote extensively and apparently
it can be demonstrated that *Science and Health*
quotes from his manuscripts. "It is demonstrably true
that Mrs. Eddy copied *thirty-three pages verbatim*
and *one hundred pages in substance* into *Science and*

Health with Key to the Scriptures, Edition 1875, from Dr. Lieber's manuscript on the writings of Hegel."[20]

It is quite obvious to any serious student that much of the material in Christian Science is not original with Mary Baker Eddy but can be found in the writings of men who pre-dated her. This is not important by itself because almost all writers are quite ready to admit the fact that they have based their work on the foundations that have been laid by others. However, it becomes vitally important in the case of Christian Science because the Founder claims unequivocally that this was a direct revelation to her and was not based on the ideas of others.

"This knowledge came to me in an hour of great need; and I give it to you as death-bed testimony to the daystar that dawned on the night of material sense. This knowledge is practical, for it wrought my immediate recovery from an injury caused by an accident, and pronounced fatal by the physicians. On the third day thereafter, I called for my Bible, and opened it at Matthew 9:2. As I read, the healing Truth dawned upon my sense; and the result was that I rose, dressed myself, and ever after was in better health than I had before enjoyed."[21]

This is a moving testimony but apparently the doctor who attended her at the time did not confirm her story. Dr. Alvin M. Cushing made an affidavit on August 13, 1904 in which he said that he did not at any time declare her to be in a critical condition or that she only had a few days to live. He went on to say that she did not say or pretend to say that she had recovered miraculously on the third day.[22]

Anyone who studies Christian Science seriously should remember that the philosophy is the idealism of Berkeley, the mental therapy is to be found in

Plato, Mesmer and Quimby, the idea of God is
Hegelian and the testimony that was supposed to
have been the basis of the system is highly
questionable.

The Scriptures

These perversions of the Christian Faith can gain
attention from church orientated people only by
giving the impression that they too are based upon
the Bible. In this respect, Christian Science is no
different.

"As adherents of Truth, we take the inspired Word
of the Bible as our sufficient guide to eternal Life."[2 3]

"The Bible has been my only authority. I have had
no other guide in 'the straight and narrow way' of
Truth."[2 4]

Of course these are the sort of statements that
appeal to Christians, but the fact of the matter is that
the Founder of Christian Science had grave misgivings
about the reliability of the Bible. "The decisions by
vote of Church Councils as to what should and should
not be considered Holy Writ; the manifest mistakes in
the ancient versions; the thirty thousand different
readings in the Old Testament, and the three hundred
thousand in the New,—these facts show how a mortal
and material sense stole into the divine record, with
its own hue darkening to some extent the inspired
pages."[2 5]

This is the age-old trick of attempting to disparage
the authority of the Bible by pointing out the
changes that have been made over a period of
hundreds of years as a result of careful scholarship
and the discovery of more ancient manuscripts. The
deception in this kind of argument is to emphasize
the changes without pointing out the nature of those
changes—that they do not alter the meaning of the

text or the doctrine but simply the terminology with which these are expressed. In fact the overwhelming similarities between all of the various versions of the Bible are much more striking than their minor differences of phraseology. Even the extremely Liberal New Curriculum of The United Church of Canada is forced to admit that the translations we have today are substantially like their original manuscripts: "No books have ever been so closely scrutinized by able and devoted men as those which we have in the Bible, and today, we are reasonably sure what the original was like."[26]

When she refers to the story in the Gospel of Mark about how Jesus healed the blind man, she says: "To suppose that Jesus did actually anoint the blind man's eyes with his spittle, is as absurd as to think, according to the report of some, that Christian Scientists sit in back-to-back seances with their patients, for the divine power to filter from vertebrae to vertebrae."[27]

When she talks about the Creation Story, she takes the modernistic position that there are two different accounts in the first and second chapters of Genesis. "The Science of the first record proves the falsity of the second. If one is true, the other is false, for they are antagonistic."[28]

One does not read the official textbooks of the Christian Science Church without realizing very soon that their author leans for support upon the Bible when it suits her purpose but denies it when it obviously contradicts her ideas.

Entirely apart from this expression of her lack of confidence in the authority of the Bible, the doctrines of Christian Science make it apparently evident that Mrs. Eddy was quite willing to violate every major doctrine that has been accepted by the

Christian Church as the obvious teaching of the Bible throughout its entire history. Four examples of this will serve our purpose.

God

In Christian Science, God is not personal in any sense but is described as Principle, Invisible Good, Mind, etc.

In stark contrast to the impersonal god of Christian Science, the Bible presents a very personal God. He remembers (Isaiah 43:25), He speaks (Isaiah 42:8), He hears (Exodus 2:24), He sees (Genesis 6:5), He knows (II Timothy 2:19), and He judges (Ezekiel 34:20). The author of the Book of Hebrews introduces his epistle by equating Jesus Christ and God and describing God as a Person: "Who being the brightness of his glory, and the express image of his person" (Hebrews 1:3).

The Atonement

Christian Science refuses to accept the Biblical doctrine of the Atonement: "The material blood of Jesus was no more efficacious to cleanse from sin when it was shed upon 'the accursed tree,' than when it was flowing in his veins as he went daily about his Father's business."[29]

Even a casual student of the Bible knows that it flatly contradicts Christian Science at this point: "Having made peace through the blood of his cross, by him to reconcile all things unto himself; by him, I say, whether they be things in earth, or things in heaven" (Colossians 1:20). The Apostle John reiterates the same truth when he says, "The blood of Jesus Christ his Son cleanseth us from all sin" (I John 1:7).

Sin

If we were forced to condense the message of the entire Bible into one or two sentences, we might say that it is written to reveal the fact of sin and the way of salvation. However, Christian Science refuses to admit the existence of sin. "To get rid of sin through Science, is to divest sin of any supposed mind or reality . . . Man is incapable of sin."[30]

The Bible states quite clearly: "If we say that we have no sin, we deceive ourselves, and the truth is not in us . . . If we say that we have not sinned, we make him a liar, and his word is not in us (I John 1:8 and 10).

Jesus Christ

Christian Science conceives of Jesus as an idea not a person and it makes a distinction between Christ and Jesus.

"The Virgin-mother conceived this idea of God, and gave to her ideal the name of Jesus . . . the eternal Christ and the corporeal Jesus manifest in flesh, continued until the Master's ascension, when the human, material concept, or Jesus, disappeared . . . A portion of God could not enter man; neither could God's fulness be reflected by a single man . . . Jesus is the name of the man who, more than all other men, has presented Christ, the true idea of God."[31]

Once again Christian Science chooses to deliberately contradict the teaching of the Bible in regard to Jesus Christ. "Hereby know ye the Spirit of God: Every spirit that confesseth that Jesus Christ is come in the flesh is of God: And every spirit that confesseth not that Jesus Christ is come in the flesh is not of God: and this is that spirit of anti-christ, whereof ye have heard that it should come; and even now already is it in the world" (I John 4:2–3).

The Bible says that in Jesus Christ "dwelleth all the fulness of the Godhead bodily" (Colossians 2:9).

One final verse along this line will suffice. "Who is a liar but he that denieth that Jesus is the Christ? He is antichrist, that denieth the Father and the Son" (I John 2:22).

Conclusion

The Bible accepts the fact of the creation of the material world by God. It declares the actual existence of sin, suffering, disease and death. If, as Mrs. Eddy suggests, all of these are error, one would think that the Bible would be the place where this falsehood would be explained every time it occurred. However, the Bible never once gives this explanation.

The only book that does is *Science and Health with Key to the Scriptures.* In view of this fact, either this book is infinitely superior to the Bible because it goes far beyond it by explaining the error of sin, suffering, disease and death, or else the Christian Science textbook is based upon a false assumption that is a direct contradiction of the Bible.

Those who accept the absolute authority of the Bible cannot accept *Science and Health,* and those who believe the teachings of *Science and Health* must reject the message of the Bible.

FOOTNOTES

[1] Hoekema, *The Four Major Cults,* p. 180.
[2] Census of Canada, pp. 41–1 and 45–17.
[3] Mary Baker Eddy, *Science and Health with Key to the Scriptures* (Boston, 1934), p. 123.
[4] Ibid., p. 372.

[5] Mary Baker Eddy, *Miscellaneous Writings* (Boston, 1924), p. 47.

[6] Eddy, *Science and Health,* p. 425.

[7] Ibid., pp. 221–222.

[8] Ibid., p. 176.

[9] Ibid., p. 194.

[10] Ibid., p. 153.

[11] Ibid., p. 107.

[12] Ibid., p. 110.

[13] Ibid., p. 126.

[14] Arthur Kenyon Rogers, *A Student's History of Philosophy* (New York: The MacMillan Company, 1942), p. 316.

[15] *The Republic*, Book III, section 408, p. 337.

[16] Hoekema, *The Four Major Cults,* p. 177.

[17] Walter R. Martin, *The Kingdom of the Cults* (Grand Rapids: Zondervan Publishing House, 1966), pp. 111 and 112.

[18] Lyman P. Powell, *Mary Baker Eddy—A Life Size Portrait* (Boston: Christian Science Publishing House, 1950), pp. 96, 97 and 98.

[19] Hoekema, *The Four Major Cults,* p. 173.

[20] *Martin,* The Kindgom of the Cults pp. 112–113.

[21] Eddy, *Miscellaneous Writings,* p. 24.

[22] Hoekema, *The Four Major Cults,* p. 174.

[23] Eddy, *Science and Health,* p. 497.

[24] Ibid., p. 126.

[25] Ibid., p. 139.

[26] Thomson, *God and His Purpose,* p. 41.

[27] Eddy, *Miscellaneous Writings,* p. 171.

[28] Eddy, *Science and Health,* p. 522.

[29] Ibid., p. 25.

[30] Ibid., pp. 339 and 475.

[31] Ibid., pp. 29, 334, 336 and 473.

CHAPTER IX

THE ARMSTRONG POLYCULT

The Christian religion may be the most dogmatic in the world. It is impossible to be faithful to the teaching of the Bible and at the same time make room for any other faith. Any man who accepts the absolute authority of the Scriptures believes that there is no other way to God except through faith in Jesus Christ.

Jesus was dogmatic when He said: "I am the way, the truth, and the life: no man cometh unto the Father, but by me" (John 14:6).

The Apostle Peter was simply reaffirming this position when he declared: "Neither is there salvation in any other: for there is none other name under heaven given among men, whereby we must be saved" (Acts 4:12).

The Apostle Paul restated exactly the same thing when he wrote: "For there is one God, and one mediator between God and men, the man Christ Jesus" (I Timothy 2:5).

The Bible emphasizes the exclusiveness of the Gospel of Jesus Christ but nowhere does it suggest that there will ever be a time when there will be no one in the world preaching the Gospel or when God will be limited to the preaching of one man and his associates. All of the traditional denominations and churches that have accepted the Bible as their only authority have recognized the fact that they are not alone in the preaching of the Gospel. This is what makes the existence of inter-denominational organizations a possibility and there are scores of them;

140

Gideons, Youth for Christ, Christian Business Men's Committees, Campus Crusade, Inter-Varsity, and dozens of faith missionary societies depend on the support of people from all of the denominations and churches. No Bible-believing church deludes itself into thinking that it is the only church preaching the Gospel.

"Incredible Though It Seems"

To use one of Herbert W. Armstrong's cliches, "incredible though it seems" he actually believes that his Radio Church of God is the only place where the Gospel is being preached today, that *The Plain Truth* magazine is the only one that is publishing the Gospel and that his Ambassador Colleges are the only schools that provide a proper education. Furthermore, he thinks that until the Armstrongs burst on the American religious scene, there was no one in the world preaching the Gospel—that for more than eighteen centuries the Gospel message has been buried.

The Armstrong Family

In the year 1969 Herbert W. Armstrong was approximately seventy-seven years of age. His wife who had been responsible for leading him into a great deal of his teaching died in 1967. His son, Garner Ted, is following in his father's footsteps and it would seem that he has the same magnetic voice and personality and is responsible for the majority of the work today. It is almost impossible to tell the difference between father and son on the radio broadcasts.

"The World Tomorrow"

The Armstrong broadcasts can be heard almost twenty-four hours a day throughout North America and in more than thirty-five countries of the world. In April of 1969 the radio log listed approximately 310 stations. Most of these were in the United States but "The World Tomorrow" could be heard from coast to coast in Canada on forty-three different radio stations. In the City of Toronto two major stations carried his broadcasts and in addition he had four programmes in the French language, two in German and one in Italian.[1]

Each broadcast is thirty minutes in length and is nothing but preaching from beginning to end. However, both of the Armstrongs have remarkable radio voices and they speak in a manner that captivates the interest of almost anybody. In addition to the radio outlets, "The World Tomorrow" is telecast on twenty-seven stations—fifteen of them in Canada.[2]

The Plain Truth

The cover of the Armstrong magazine is almost identical to *Time* or *Newsweek* and the entire format is very sharp, most contemporary and probably much more costly than either *Time* or *Newsweek* because of the full colour prints that are carried throughout its pages.

It is published monthly with forty-eight pages and in 1969 boasted a circulation of 1,650,000 copies.[3]

What's The Attraction?

Undoubtedly the magnetism of Herbert W. Armstrong's teaching is in at least two areas. As is true of every other cult, probably more than fifty per cent of his teaching is good. Christians who accept the absolute authority of the Bible respond to his strong stand against the theory of evolution and his constant opposition to the New Morality, to say nothing of his continual reiteration about his belief in the Bible.

The second attraction of the Armstrong cult is his emphasis on the sad state of affairs in the modern world and his promise of life in the world of tomorrow.

The Super Egotist

In a personal letter dated November 27, 1958, Armstrong declared unequivocally that his work was the only one preaching the Gospel of the Bible and that it was a fulfillment of Jesus' prophecy, "And this gospel of the kingdom shall be preached in all the world for a witness unto all nations; and then shall the end come" (Matthew 24:14).

Here are Armstrong's words: "You have a right to know all about this great work of God—and about me. First, let me say—this may sound incredible, but it's true—Jesus Christ foretold this very work—It is, itself, the fulfillment of His prophecy (Matthew 24:14 and Mark 13:10) . . . Astounding as it may seem, there is no other work on earth proclaiming to the whole world this very same Gospel that Jesus taught and proclaimed."[4]

This statement automatically rules out the effectiveness of every preacher of the Gospel from the time of the disciples throughout nearly nineteen centuries. None of the early church fathers, none of the Roman Catholics during the Middle Ages, none of the Reformers and none of the modern revival leaders and evangelists preached the Gospel. When a person embraces the teaching of Herbert Armstrong, he must at the same time accept the incredible concept that men like Martin Luther, John Knox, John Wesley, General William Booth, Dwight L. Moody, Billy Graham, John Stott and C.S. Lewis did not understand nor preach the Gospel.

The Ambassador Colleges

In addition to eliminating all of the great Christian leaders of the past and present, if a man accepts the Armstrong gospel, he must also cross off every educational institution apart from the three Ambassador Colleges in Texas, California and England.

"Today, incredible though it sound, the student cannot obtain what he really needs anywhere except on one of the three Ambassador College campuses."[5]

"God wants us to add to our fund of knowledge whatever man can correctly discover for himself. That is the real purpose of schools and colleges. But how many institutions are based on these principles? As far as we know, only the three campuses of Ambassador College."[6]

Thus the Armstrong devotee must recognize that no denominational or inter-denominational institution offers a proper Christian education. According to Armstrong, there are only three places in the entire world where you can be adequately educated. Two of them are in the United States and one is in England. This means that most of the continents and countries of the world have no proper educational facilities. This would include India, Asia, South America, Australia, New Zealand, Africa and Continental Europe. My country, Canada, is one of the many places in the world where it would be absolutely impossible for us to be properly educated.

Of course, Armstrong's answer to this would be the Ambassador College Correspondence Course which is available in most of these countries. *The Plain Truth* makes the same claims for it as it does for the Ambassador Colleges: "When it comes to learning the answers to the really important questions of life, there exists a tremendous 'knowledge gap.' There is only one educational institution on earth which is filling this incredible gap. Besides producing The World Tomorrow educational radio and TV programs and printing the magazine you are now reading, it also publishes the Ambassador College Correspondence Course. This course is published as part of the worldwide educational program of Ambassador College."[7]

The Only Magazine

In the area of literature you can read the Gospel in only one place—the Armstrong publications.

"There is only one publishing work on earth today that is filling this incredible gap. It prints the magazine you are now reading—*The Plain Truth.*

"The Plain Truth is able to give you knowledge unobtainable elsewhere because it recognizes that the foundations of all knowledge is the Word of God—the Bible.

"It prints information absolutely unobtainable elsewhere. It reveals human nature for what it is.

"The Plain Truth reveals how to change human nature—how to overcome its downward pull through the power of God's Holy Spirit.

"This knowledge is basic. It is vital.

"You can get it from no other source.

"Yes, *The Plain Truth* has answered question after question that millions of people had never heard answered before. And it speaks with authority.

"And always those answers came right out of the Bible.

"Where else on the face of this earth could you receive such knowledge and understanding?"[8]

Most intelligent people need only to read this much of the Armstrong "truth" and they dismiss him and his organizations from any further consideration.

However, there are thousands of people who are impressed by the smooth talk of a super egotist and just as men like Adolf Hitler and Benito Mussolini led thousands of their followers to physical destruction, so men like Herbert W. Armstrong may lead thousands to spiritual destruction.

Such people will listen to The World Tomorrow broadcasts and read *The Plain Truth* magazine for months without realizing what's wrong. One of the reasons for this is that the Armstrongs take an incredibly long time to get to their point and in the course of all the good talk and writing that leads up to the point, one is quite likely to miss the error of the point itself. The message of the Radio Church of God seems to be a weird and intricate mixture of the teachings of British Israelites, Jehovah's Witnesses, Mormons and Seventh Day Adventists. In a nutshell, Armstrong's prophecy is British Israelism. His way of salvation represents a distortion of Seventh Day Adventism. His view of God is to be found in the teaching of the Mormon Church and his doctrine of the next world is almost exactly the same as that of Jehovah's Witnesses.

Prophecy—British Israelism

Although Armstrong's prophecy seems to be an exact replica of British Israelism, it would be unfair to associate the British Israelites with the rest of his doctrine. For the most part those who hold this particular prophetic position are otherwise sound on the basic doctrines of the Bible and are seldom considered to be members of a false cult. Carried to an extreme, British Israelism can deteriorate into a sort of national salvation instead of a personal experience with Jesus Christ.

In his 226-page book on the subject, Armstrong

puts it this way: "Whoever is Ephraim and Manasseh today must have been in possession of the earth's choicest agricultural, mineral, and other wealth—the great gold and silver mines; iron, oil, and coal, timber and other resources.

"What nations fulfill these prophecies? Why, only Great Britain and America!

"If we are not national Israel—so called 'lost' Ten Tribes—prosperous Joseph—Israel—Birthright Israel— actual inheritors of the Birthright blessings which were to be bestowed beginning 1803 A.D., then who else can be?"[9]

In short, the British Israelite theory is that the lost Ten Tribes of Israel are now the English speaking peoples of the world. In particular, Great Britain is Ephraim and the United States is Manesseh. The monarch of the British throne is thought to be a direct descendant of King David and all of the promises to Israel are to be fulfilled in Great Britain and the United States—not in a national Israel.

On the surface at least there are two factors that are an embarrassment to modern British Israelites. One is that the fantastic days of the British Empire are now over and Great Britain is no longer the major power in the world. There is little question in anyone's mind that the United States is one of the big powers and the other is no longer Great Britain but Russia and the communistic nations. As a matter of fact, there are those who would question whether Great Britain even stands in third place today. Certainly Japan, West Germany and several of the other European countries might very well stand third or fourth on the list.

In the second place the present monarch of Great Britain happens to be a Queen rather than the King promised by the Old Testament: "There shall not fail thee a man upon the throne of Israel" (I Kings 9:5).

When the British Israelites quote passages such as this to support their concept that the British throne is indeed the continuation of the Throne of David, they conveniently ignore the fact that God's promises are generally conditional. In this passage God is speaking to King Solomon and the Bible says this: "If thou wilt walk before me, as David thy father walked, in integrity of heart, and in uprightness to do according to all that I have commanded thee, and wilt keep my statutes and my judgments: Then I will establish the throne of thy kingdom upon Israel for ever, as I promised to David thy father, saying, There shall not fail thee a man upon the throne of Israel" (I Kings 9:4—5).

A New Discovery

The Armstrongs teach the prophecy of British Israelism as if no one had ever heard of it before they came along: "Yet the best minds in the world are in total ignorance of the unprecedented cataclysm that is about to strike!

"And why have these prophecies not been understood, or believed?

"Because the vital key that unlocks prophecy to our understanding had been lost. That key is the identity of the United States and the British peoples in Biblical prophecy.

"That key has been found!

"We present it to those whose unprejudiced eyes are willing to see, in this book."[10]

Anyone who has had any sort of religious education at all is quite aware of the fact that the doctrine of British Israelism can be traced back for at least four hundred years to Counsellor Le Loyer of France who wrote a book called *The Ten Lost Tribes*

Found in the year 1590. In 1723 Dr. Abbadie of Amsterdam wrote, "The ten tribes must be sought for in the North and West and in the British Isles." In 1840 John Wilson wrote the classic on the subject *Our Israelitish Origin*.

No Scholastic Backing

In the eleventh edition of *The Encyclopaedia Britannica* published in 1910 there is a short article under the caption "Anglo–Israelite Theory" which concludes with this statement: "The theory (which is fully set forth in a book called *Philo–Israel*) rests on premises which are deemed by scholars—both theological and anthropological—to be utterly unsound."[1] In the 1967 edition British Israelism does not seem to be mentioned at all.

J. Oswald Sanders says: "So far as we are aware, no competent and reputable historian has identified himself with the movement."[12]

In a fifty-one page treatise on the Armstrong cult, Robert G. Grant puts it this way: "A classic quotation on this topic comes from the excellent and authoritative book entitled, *The Monuments and the Old Testament*. Its authors are Dr. Maurice Price, Professor of Semitic Languages and Literatures at the University of Chicago; Dr. Ovid Sellers, archeologist and Professor of Old Testament Language at McCormack Theological Seminary; and Dr. E. Leslie Carlson, Professor of Old Testament at Southwestern Theological Seminary . . . the authors observed: . . . 'there is no people or nation or tongue today that can be identified as the lost ten tribes'."[13]

One of the premises of British Israelism is that the Israelites or the ten tribes did not return to Palestine after their captivity but wandered through Continental Europe to the British Isles and hence to the

United States. Armstrong says that none of the ten tribes returned to Palestine after the captivity: "Consequently those in Jerusalem in the time of Christ were of these three tribes, not of the House of Israel."[1 4]

The writers of the Old Testament recognize no such permanent division of the twelve tribes but rather refer to them interchangeably as Jews and as Israel. This is apparent in the Books of Ezra, Nehemiah, Zechariah and Amos. Conservative scholarship is unanimous in dating Ezra, Nehemiah and Zechariah after the years of captivity and although Amos prophesied in the Northern Kingdom just before the captivity, he is quite clear in predicting the ultimate restoration of the Israelites (Amos 9:11–15).

Nor do the New Testament writers recognize such a division. The names Israel and Jew are used interchangeably. In the third chapter of John, Nicodemus is referred to as "a ruler of the Jews" and "a master of Israel" (John 3:1 & 10). Reference to the tribes usually recognizes no distinction. Standing before King Agrippa the Apostle Paul said: "Unto which promise our twelve tribes, instantly serving God day and night, hope to come" (Acts 26:7).

On the Day of Pentecost the Apostle Peter demonstrated an appalling degree of ignorance about the British Israelite theory when he bunched all of the tribes together in these words: "Therefore let all the house of Israel know assuredly, that God hath made that same Jesus, whom ye have crucified, both Lord and Christ" (Acts 2:36).

The Apostle James referred to all of the tribes as being scattered: "James, a servant of God and of the Lord Jesus Christ, to the twelve tribes which are scattered abroad, greeting" (James 1:1).

Herbert Armstrong tries desperately to make a distinction between the House of Israel and the Kingdom of Israel and thus get himself off the Biblical hook which obviously indicates that there were representatives of all twelve tribes in Palestine during the days of Jesus. Even if we were to concede that members of the Northern Kingdom did not return to Palestine, the theory of British Israelism would still fail to stand the test of Biblical revelation because it depends upon this kingdom turning up eventually as a unit in Great Britain, whereas the Bible describes them along with all the other tribes as being scattered throughout the nations: "For, lo, I will command, and I will sift the house of Israel among all nations, like as corn is sifted in a sieve, yet shall not the least grain fall upon the earth" (Amos 9:9).

Armstrong's Salvation

Armstrong's salvation is in two parts. For the first part he uses the term *justification* which in his vocabulary has very little similarity to the same word as it is used in the Bible. It is accomplished by repenting and turning to Christ but it involves only the sin of the past.

For the second part he uses the word *salvation* and once again he is forced to re-define it in a manner that is quite different from its use in the Bible. Salvation is accomplished by keeping the Ten Commandments and does not occur until the resurrection.

Herbert Armstrong is quite open in his complete contradiction of the teaching in the New Testament, particularly by the Apostle Paul. He states emphatically that salvation involves faith and works: "But how the god of this world would blind your eyes to that!

He tries to deceive you into thinking all there is to it is just 'accepting Christ,'—with 'no works'—and presto-chango, you're pronounced 'saved'!"[15]

In attempting to describe what constitutes a Christian, *The Plain Truth* says: "The key to happiness is a willing, wholehearted obedience to God's living law of love—the Ten Commandments ... Unless and until you actively begin to obey all ten of God's Commandments, in the spirit as well as in the letter, you will not—you cannot—experience true happiness ... A person who is practicing all seven of these principles would be continually giving his life in service to God and man; he would be obeying God's Commandments; he would have repented of his guilty past and quit sinning; he would be growing in his understanding of God's plan; he would be striving to build God-like character; he would have a healthy fear of God; and he would be trusting God, in living faith, to work out his problems. Such a person would be a Christian!"[16]

The Answer

The Apostle Paul answered the question of faith and works in many different passages in the Bible but perhaps one of the clearest is the third chapter of Galatians. The entire chapter should be read and studied but the first five verses establish the theme: "O you dear idiots of Galatia, who saw Jesus Christ the crucified so plainly, who has been casting a spell over you? I will ask you one simple question: did you receive the Spirit of God by trying to keep the Law or by believing the message of the Gospel? Surely you can't be so idiotic as to think that a man begins his spiritual life in the Spirit and then completes it by reverting to outward observances? Has all your painful experience brought you nowhere? I simply cannot believe it of you! Does God, Who gives you His Spirit and works miracles among you, do these things because you have obeyed the Law or because you have believed the Gospel? Ask yourselves that."[1][7]

This is only one of many similar passages in the writings of the Apostle Paul establishing the principle again and again that salvation is a result of faith plus nothing. As a matter of fact, Paul says the same thing so many times in so many different ways that it is impossible to doubt his meaning. However, as soon as anyone quotes passages like this the followers of Armstrong will begin to shout at the top of their lungs about the Book of James.

This is the only major passage in the Bible that would seem to make works part of the way of salvation: "Even so faith, if it hath not works, is dead, being alone. Yea, a man may say, Thou hast faith, and I have works: shew me thy faith without thy works, and I will shew thee my faith by my works . . . Was not Abraham our father justified by works, when he had offered Isaac his son upon the altar? Seest thou how faith wrought with his works, and by works was faith made perfect? And the scripture was fulfilled which saith, Abraham believed God, and it was imputed unto him for righteousness: and he was called the Friend of God. Ye see then how that by works a man is justified, and not by faith only" (James 2:17–18, 21–24).

No Contradiction

It should be understood that the Bible does not contradict itself and certainly whatever may be the meaning of this difficult passage in James, we may assume that he is not contradicting the teaching of the Apostle Paul. Both men were inspired by the

Holy Spirit and the Bible makes it clear that in such a situation they must agree with one another or else we may conclude that one is not inspired by God at all. The Apostle Paul puts it this way: "For God is not the author of confusion, but of peace, as in all churches of the saints" (I Corinthians 14:33).

In the epistles of Paul we are confronted primarily with the problem of Judaism and the resulting legalism and thus the Apostle reiterates many times the fact that man does not assist God in his salvation. He is saved by grace through faith and therefore has no reason whatsoever to boast. "For by grace are ye saved through faith; and that not of yourselves: it is the gift of God: Not of works, lest any man should boast" (Ephesians 2:8—9).

The Apostle James is dealing with a different problem entirely—the problem of the person who uses the grace of God as a licence to sin. This is antinomianism—a word used by the Reformers to describe such a person.

The key to this passage in James is in verse eighteen, "Yea, a man may say, Thou hast faith, and I have works: shew me thy faith without thy works, and I will shew thee my faith by my works" (James 2:18).

James is obviously talking about justification before other people. Certainly a man does not have to demonstrate his faith before God in order to prove it. God sees the heart and knows whether there is any real living faith with or without works. However, other people cannot see a man's heart and the only way that they can determine whether a person's faith is real is by his works and if there are no works, other people have every right to conclude that there is no faith either or that his faith is dead.

Every major commentator who understands the

ancient languages and is cognizant of the complete teaching of the New Testament is quite aware of the problem that seems to exist between Paul and James, but without exception they recognize the fact that there is no real problem if one thoroughly understands the Scriptures.

"The justification by works of this Epistle is justification before man by furnishing to him that which he can see. God needs no such evidence, for He can read the heart and see if it is animated by a living faith. The source of justification is grace; the ground, atonement; the means, faith; and the evidence, works. The Epistle to the Romans deals with the first three; the Epistle of James with the last."[18]

"Faith cooperated with his works (v. 22) and was perfected by them, we may say, as the tree is perfected by its fruits, which show that the tree is a living tree . . . If says Ropes, when the test came, the faith had not been matched by works, then it would have been proved to be an incomplete faith . . . not a faith severed from works, but a faith which proves its reality and vitality in works. According to a saying of the Reformers, we are justified by faith alone, but not by the faith that is alone."[19]

"Paul, in Romans and Galatians, fights against self-righteousness; James, in this Epistle, contends against formalism and licentiousness. James's 'faith without works' is not the justifying faith of Romans 3:28—'working through love'; it is rather the useless faith without love of which Paul speaks in I Corinthians 13."[20]

The Apostle Paul did not ignore the problem of Anti-nomianism. After establishing the doctrine of salvation by faith without works, he then asks the question, "What shall we say then? Shall we continue in sin, that grace may abound?" (Romans 6:1). Paul's answer to this question is not that a man must keep the Ten Commandments in a legalistic fashion but rather that he should yield himself completely to Jesus Christ who gives us the power to live a godly life.

"For sin shall not have dominion over you; for ye are not under the law, but under grace . . . Being then made free from sin, ye became the servants of righteousness" (Romans 6:14 & 18).

Summary

The Bible makes it remarkably clear that man is saved by grace through faith plus nothing. This concept appears so many times in the New Testament that it cannot be doubted. After a man has been saved by faith, there should be some evidence of the reality of his experience that can be seen by other people. The Apostle Paul called this evidence the fruit of the Spirit. The Apostle James calls this evidence works. In other words, God knows a man is justified by his faith. Other people are aware of the fact that a man is justified because of his works or the fruits of the Spirit that are demonstrated in his life.

Armstrong obviously developed his gospel from his early associations with off-shoots of the Seventh Day Adventist Church. However, it would be totally unfair to modern Seventh Day Adventists to say that Armstrong's way of salvation and their doctrine of salvation are the same.

Life After Death

Along with Jehovah's Witnesses, The World Tomorrow teaches that man does not have an immortal soul and there is no such thing as eternal punishment.

"The wages you are going to be paid for having

sinned is death! Then why do so many religious people teach exactly the opposite of the Bible—why do they teach that the wages of sin is eternal life in hell? . . . We teach eternal punishment. That punishment, your Bible says, is not eternal life in a hellfire of endless torture—not eternal punishing—eternal punishment—it is death for eternity."[2][1]

The only answer that is really necessary to this distortion of Biblical teaching is the story that Jesus told of the rich man and Lazarus (Luke 16). In this passage He establishes the fact of another life apart from this world entirely where two different kinds of men live in two different states—one in torment and the other in blessedness. The only way that one can get around this passage is by an elaborate system of symbolism that is not warranted in the simple story told by Jesus—and which is not supported by the rest of His teaching.

Other Passages

"And they will go away to eternal punishment, but the righteous will enter eternal life" (Matthew 25:46, The New English Bible).

"The curse is upon you; go from my sight to the eternal fire that is ready for the devil and his angels" (Matthew 25:41, The New English Bible).

"Whoever worships the beast and its image and receives its mark on his forehead or hand, he shall drink the wine of God's wrath, poured undiluted into the cup of vengeance. He shall be tormented in sulphurous flames before the holy angels and before the Lamb. The smoke of their torment will rise for ever and ever, and there will be no respite day or night for those who worship the beast and its image or receive the mark of its name" (Revelation 14:9—11, The New English Bible).

These are only a few examples of the very clear

teaching of the Bible regarding the reality of eternal
punishment for the unsaved.

No Soul—No Heaven

"Why is it that religious people speak continually
about 'your mortal soul,' about 'going to heaven,'
about dead loved ones being now 'with the Lord,' and
many other such things supposed to be the basic
beliefs of Christianity—and yet never once showing
you any such teaching in the Bible! They talk of
these teachings as if they were true. They lead you to
take these teachings for granted—to suppose they
came from the Bible."[2 2]

The best way to answer this accusation is to let the
Bible speak for itself: "For I am in a strait betwixt
two, having a desire to depart, and to be with Christ;
which is far better" (Philippians 1:23).

"For we know that if our earthly house of this
tabernacle were dissolved, we have a building of God,
an house not made with hands, eternal in the heavens.
For in this we groan, earnestly desiring to be clothed
upon with our house which is from heaven: If so be
that being clothed we shall not be found naked. For
we that are in this tabernacle do groan, being
burdened: not for that we would be unclothed, but
clothed upon, that mortality might be swallowed up
of life. Now he that hath wrought us for the selfsame
thing is God, who also hath given unto us the earnest
of the Spirit. Therefore we are always confident,
knowing that, whilst we are at home in the body, we
are absent from the Lord: (For we walk by faith, not
by sight:) We are confident, I say, and willing rather
to be absent from the body, and to be present with
the Lord" (II Corinthians 5:1—8).

Obviously, the Apostle Paul expected that his
death would usher him immediately into the presence
of his Lord and he said so on several occasions.

"Let not your heart be troubled: ye believe in God, believe also in me. In my Father's house are many mansions: if it were not so, I would have told you. I go to prepare a place for you. And if I go and prepare a place for you, I will come again, and receive you unto myself; that where I am, there ye may be also. And whither I go ye know, and the way ye know" (John 14:1—4).

Conclusion

These are the basic errors of the Armstrong cult and the Biblical answers to them. "It has been wisely observed that men are at liberty to reject Jesus Christ and the Bible as the Word of God; they are at liberty to oppose Him; they are at liberty to challenge it. But they are not at liberty to alter the essential message of the Scriptures, which is the good news that God does care for the lost souls of His children, and so loved us as to send His only Son that we might live through Him."[23]

FOOTNOTES

[1] *The Plain Truth,* "Radio Log", April 1969, pp. 21—23, Vol. XXXIV, No. 4.

[2] Ibid.

[3] Ibid., Inside Cover.

[4] Robert L. Sumner, *Herbert W. Armstrong, A False Prophet* (Murfreesboro: Sword of the Lord Foundation, 1961), p. 4.

[5] Herbert W. Armstrong, "What Colleges and Universities Do Not Tell You", *The Plain Truth,* April 1967, p. 6, Vol. XXXII, No. 4.

[6] Herman L. Hoeh, "Education Without God", *The Plain Truth,* February 1967, p. 26, Vol. XXXII, No. 2.

[7] Richard H. Sedliacik, "How Ambassador College Fills Today's Knowledge Gap", *The Plain Truth,* February 1969, p. 29, Vol. XXXIV, No. 2.

[8] Eugene M. Walter, "How the Plain Truth Fills

Today's Knowledge Gap", *The Plain Truth,* February 1967, pp. 29, 30 and 31.

[9] Herbert W. Armstrong, *The United States and British Commonwealth in Prophecy* (Pasadena: Ambassador College Press, 1967) pp. 175, 179 and 180.

[10] Ibid., p. xii.

[11] *Encyclopaedia Britannica* (New York: The Encyclopaedia Britannica Company, 1911), Vol. 2, p.31.

[12] J. Oswald Sanders, *Cults & Isms* (Grand Rapids: Zondervan Publishing House, 1962), p. 139.

[13] Robert G. Grant, *The Plain Truth About the Armstrong Cult* (Glendale: The California Graduate School of Theology, 1969), pp. 33–34.

[14] Armstrong, *The United States and British Commonwealth in Prophecy,* p. 92.

[15] Herbert W. Armstrong, *Why Were You Born?* (Pasadena: Ambassador College, 1957), p. 11.

[16] Eugene M. Walter, "Here's How You Can Be Happy", *The Plain Truth,* January 1967, pp. 30, 31 and 32, Vol. XXXII, No. 1.

[17] J. B. Phillips, *Letters to Young Churches* (New York: The MacMillan Company, 1951), Gal. 3:1–5, pp. 95–96.

[18] George Williams, *The Student's Commentary on the Holy Scriptures* (Grand Rapids: Kiegel Publications, 1956), p. 994.

[19] *The New International Commentary on the New Testament,* Alexander Ross, *Commentary on the Epistles of James and John* (Grand Rapids: Wm. B. Eerdmans Publishing Company, 1964), pp. 54–55.

[20] *The Pulpit Commentary* (Grand Rapids: Wm. B. Eerdmans Publishing Company, 1950), Vol. 21, p. 38.

[21] Herbert W. Armstrong, "What Do You Mean . . . Salvation?", *The Plain Truth,* December 1966, pp. 10 and 13, Vol. XXXI, No. 12.

[22] Ibid., p. 10.

[23] Martin, *The Kingdom of the Cults,* p. 14.